D1606248

THE TOP 300
SURNAMES
OF
DERRY-LONDONDERRY

By
Brian Mitchell

Maps by
Sam Mitchell

CLEARFIELD

Copyright © 2017 by
Brian Mitchell

Printed for Clearfield Company by
Genealogical Publishing Company
Baltimore, Maryland
2017

ISBN 978-0-8063-5842-0

Made in the United States of America

PREFACE

Surname Importance

An understanding of surname history is an important aid to family history. Exploring the history of your surname is a useful first step on a journey to tracing roots in Ireland. Surnames, as they are very much connected to place in Ireland, are an integral part of Irish identity and family history. Pride in Irish roots is often reflected, and indeed reinforced, in pride in surname, or an ancestor's surname, which confirms a connection with Ireland.

Surnames, or inherited family names, are the building blocks of genealogy; without them, it would be impossible to trace our ancestors back through the generations. Although only detailed family history research will confirm the actual Irish origins of your ancestors, surname histories can provide clues and insight into family origins.

The family histories associated with the surname histories in this book will, in many instances, be recorded in the database of Derry Genealogy at www.derry.rootsireland.ie. The database of Derry Genealogy contains the bulk of pre-1922 civil birth and marriage registers for the city and county of Derry, the early baptismal and marriage registers of 97 churches (the earliest being St Columb's Cathedral, inside the walled city of Londonderry, dating from 1642), gravestone inscriptions from 117 graveyards, and census substitutes and census returns dating from 1628 to 1921.

Derry or Londonderry?

Today, it is a matter of personal preference to refer to the city and county as either Derry or Londonderry.

By tradition, in 546 AD, the church of Doire [anglicised as Derry] Calgach, "the oak wood of Calgach", was founded by St Columcille, also known as St Columba, on the crest of a small, wooded hill on the west bank of the River Foyle. The original church of hewn oak, thatched with reeds, was located where St Augustine's Church stands today. For the next one thousand years Derry was a monastic centre of some importance.

The city of Londonderry, a settlement funded by the city of London, was then established on this site by royal charter of James I on 29 March 1613. By 1619 the city was completely enclosed within a stone wall, 24 feet high and 18 feet thick. This walled city assumed a pivotal role in safeguarding the settlement of 17th century English and Scottish planters as its walls repulsed Sieges in 1641, 1649 and 1689.

The charter of 1613 also defined and established a new county which was also called Londonderry. The new county of Londonderry had been enlarged, and consisted of the County of Coleraine, the heavily wooded Barony of Loughinsholin in Tyrone, the City and Liberties of Londonderry on the Donegal side of the River Foyle, and the Town and Liberties of Coleraine on the Antrim side of the River Bann.

Family historians in the United States and Canada soon realise that Derry or Londonderry as a place of origin of their ancestor can refer to the city, the county or port of departure. At the turn of the 19th century the catchment area of port of Londonderry for emigrants departing Ireland were Counties Londonderry, Donegal and Tyrone and to a lesser extent northwest Antrim and north Fermanagh. In theory, an ancestor with an address of Derry or Londonderry could have originated in this wider area. Derry was the major emigration port for northwest Ireland, i.e. the departure point for the peoples of counties Derry, Donegal and Tyrone, from c. 1680 to 1939.

From 1861 right through to 1939 ocean-going liners called at Moville (Donegal), in the deeper waters of Lough Foyle, some 18 miles downstream from Derry, to pick up emigrants who were ferried from Derry in paddle tenders. Hence in passenger manifests for this time period Londonderry and Moville are interchangeable as Moville, the embarkation point for emigrants, was effectively the outport for Londonderry.

The city's coat of arms (granted 1613) can also be controversial. The upper part of the Arms, the red cross of St. George and the sword of St. Paul, are the original arms of the city of London. The lower part displays a castle and a skeleton sitting on a mossy stone. The skeleton is believed to represent a Norman knight, Walter de Burgo, who was held captive by William de Burgo, Earl of Ulster, in a dungeon at Greencastle (Donegal) where he starved to death in 1332. The castle on the Arms is believed to be Greencastle which was built in 1305 by the 'Red Earl', Richard de Burgo, to protect the approaches to Lough Foyle and Derry. In the early years of the 14th century the Anglo-Normans acquired a tentative foothold in Inishowen (Donegal) and Derry.

Coat of Arms of Derry/Londonderry since 1613

INTRODUCTION

The 1989 Foyle Community Directory lists 1,860 unique surnames in Derry City. Each of these surnames bears a distinctive history and taken as a whole they are a record of population movements into the Derry area over the past 400 years. Derry's dynamic history can be seen in the richness and variety of her surnames.

In this book an attempt has been made to explain the origins of the top 300 surnames, each of which had 10 or more entries in the 1989 Foyle Community Directory. The three commonest names have Donegal origins with Doherty heading the way with 469 entries, followed by McLaughlin on 276 and Gallagher with 170 entries. By way of contrast 808 surnames occur only once.

To aid understanding, the surnames are classified, wherever possible, in two ways. Firstly by cultural origin and secondly by surname origin.

Cultural Origin

Generally, Derry surnames can be identified as originating from one of three distinct groupings:

1) Gaelic – either Irish or Highland Scottish.
2) English/Lowland Scottish.
3) 20th century arrivals from outside of Ireland and Britain.

Surname Origin

Surnames, furthermore, can be divided into four classes as they are generally based on or derived from one of the following:

1) The First Name of an ancestor.
2) Local Names – whether a physical feature or an actual place name.
3) Occupational Names.
4) Nicknames – Referring to a person's physical appearance, character or habits.

For easy reference the top 40 surnames in the Derry area are listed in descending order.

County maps of England and Wales, Scotland and Ireland are also included as surnames can often be identified with a particular county or number of counties.

Today surnames mean an inherited family name, originally it meant simply an additional name. In early society our ancestors had single personal names which were quite sufficient to distinguish them in small communities. As societies became more complex and officialdom was created it became essential to add a second name: in essence an early form of the National Insurance Number. These additional names or bynames were not, at first, passed on from one generation to the next. They did, however, create a stock of names which were later turned into hereditary family names.

Of great importance to the understanding of surnames in the Derry area are the differing origins and developments of surnaming systems in Irish and Highland Scottish society as compared to England and the Lowlands of Scotland.

England

The use of bynames commenced in France about the year 1000 and they were introduced to England with the Norman Conquest from 1066. Slowly these bynames were turned into hereditary family names and by 1400 all English people inherited a surname at birth.

The most noticeable characteristic of English surnames is their extraordinary number and variety. Of the 50 commonest names in England in 1856; 27 were derived from the more popular first names, 13 from occupations, 7 from localities and 3 from nicknames.

Owing to the relatively small stock of popular first names, whether of Celtic, Germanic, Scandinavia, Norman or Biblical origins, surnames based on the first name of father or other ancestor tend to be very common. By contrast surnames based on local place names are very varied owing to the vast number of different local names; the biggest set of these are based on the names of English villages.

Through both the shortening of the more popular first names into pet forms and by the addition of suffixes, known as diminutives, such as cock, kin, ot, et, un and el, the stock of surnames was greatly increased. Thus surnames such as Adcock and Hewett were created which literally meant young or little Adam and Hugh respectively. These surnames would originally have denoted either descent from, or employee of, the person named.

Wales

In Wales the stock of surnames is not large as they were, for the most part, formed from the forename of the father in the genitive case, thus John's son became Jones and Evan's son became Evans.

Lowland Scotland

The naming tradition of Lowland Scotland and the Borders of Scotland tended to develop along English lines as it was subject to English influence. For example, many Scottish surnames with origins in the Central Lowlands are habitation names derived from place names in this region.

Ireland

Ireland was one of the first countries to adopt a system of hereditary surnames which developed from a more ancient system of clan and sept names. From the 11th century each family began to adopt its own distinctive family name generally derived from the first name of an ancestor who lived in or about the 10th century.

The surname was formed by prefixing either 'Mac' (Son of) or 'O' (Grandson or descendant of) to the ancestor's name. Surnames in Ireland, therefore, tended to identify membership of a 'sept'. A sept can be identified as 'a group of persons who, or whose immediate and known ancestors, bore a common surname and inhabited the same locality'. As a consequence, Gaelic-Irish surnames are still very dominant and numerous in the very districts where their names originated.

Although Gaelic society was one of the first to adopt a system of hereditary surnames it was also one of the last to perpetuate fixed surnames. People in these societies, in the early 18th century, were often designated by their genealogies stretching back five or more generations. For example, Shane O'Neill of Shane's Castle, County Antrim, styled himself on the family vault, which he built in 1722, as 'Shane McBrien McPhelim McShane McBrien McPhelim O'Neill Esq'. Here is family history in one name stretching back over 200 years. The last-named Phelim was Felim 'The Lame' who was Prince of Clanaboy from 1529 to 1533.

Ancient Irish Genealogies

Between the fourth and seventh centuries AD, Ireland saw the emergence of new ruling dynasties and the penetration of Christianity into the country. The ancient genealogists then got to work to confirm the new status quo by assigning this expansion in much of Ulster, Leinster and Connaught to the "descendants" of Niall of the Nine Hostages, King of Tara who was slain in 405 AD.

Many of the prominent surnames of Gaelic origin in Counties Derry, Donegal and Tyrone today trace their descent from either Eoghan or Conal Gulban, two of the sons of Niall of the Nine Hostages.

Those tracing descent from Eoghan include: Brolly, Carlin, Devlin, Donnelly, Duddy, Duffy, Farren, Gormley, Hegarty, McCloskey, McLaughlin, Mellon, Mullen, O'Hagan, O'Kane, O'Neill, Quinn and Toner. From Conall Gulban: Doherty, Friel, Gallagher, McCafferty, McDaid, McDevitt and O'Donnell.

By tradition, Eoghan and Conall Gulban conquered northwest Ireland about 425 AD, and in the process captured the great hill-top fortification of Grianan of Aileach in Inishowen, County Donegal which overlooks the city of Derry and the surrounding countryside.

As kingship, in Gaelic society, was in the possession of an extended kin-group, known as the *derbfine*, in which all those males with a great-grandfather in common were eligible for kingship, each and every branch of the family tree of the dynastic kingship group had to be accounted for.

The end result is that many of the major Gaelic Irish families have reliable genealogies dating from the 6th century AD as historical fact begins to take over from origin-legend. Today the descendants of these Irish dynastic families are the oldest authenticated male-line families surviving in Europe.

Furthermore, the ancient genealogists endowed the ruling dynasties with pedigrees of kings and warriors with origin-legends in pagan times. They also constructed genealogies which connected with Christian tradition and history as revealed in the Bible. Thus the genealogies of the emerging tribal or dynastic groups were extended back to 'The Creation' and to Noah and to Adam and Eve.

Researchers with an interest in connecting surname histories with Irish mythology and Christian tradition as revealed in the Bible may be interested in my reconstruction, in Appendix 1, of the Doherty family tree back 132 generations from Ramon 'O Dogherty of Inishowen, Chief of the Name' to 'The Creation'.

In essence, in 132 steps – in 46 generations from Ramon O'Dogherty, "Chief of the Name" of Inishowen, County Donegal to Niall of the Nine Hostages, High King of Ireland 379-405 AD, and in a further 86 generations from Niall of the Nine Hostages to Adam and Eve – the Doherty family tree charts the family history of Ireland.

Highland Scotland

In the Highlands of Scotland surnames were also of Gaelic origin and were typically formed by prefixing 'Mac' (Son of) to an ancestor's name.

The Highlands were organised in a 'clan' system. As clan is an anglicised form of the Gaelic word for children it implies that every member of the clan descends from the tribal father from whom the clan derives its name. Be careful though in assuming that Scottish clan membership denotes common origins; it does not necessarily do so.

In Ireland, it is generally accepted that members of an Irish sept have a common tribal ancestor. In Scotland, a number of families, having different surnames, comprised a clan which was known by the name of the leading sept in it. Furthermore, the advisability of belonging to a large and powerful clan resulted in the assumption of the clan surname by persons who merely lived in its territory and were of no kindred to the chief.

Historical Background

Owing to its history all the above naming traditions are well represented in Derry; from the numerical strength of a small number of surnames of Gaelic-Irish origin to the great richness and variety of surnames of English and Scottish origin, where Norman-French influence held sway.

In the 12th century the Normans were the first to bring English-style surnames to Ireland. It was a series of immigrations, however, during the 17th century, coming from the Lowlands and Borders of Scotland and, to a lesser extent, from various parts of England and Wales which established a great variety of new surnames alongside the existing Gaelic-Irish ones in the Derry area.

The 17th Century Plantation of Ulster

In the 17th century substantial numbers of English and Scottish families settled in the northern part of Ireland during the so-called Plantation of Ulster. The Province of Ulster consists of the counties of Antrim, Armagh, Down, Fermanagh, Londonderry and Tyrone in Northern Ireland and the counties of Cavan, Donegal and Monaghan in the Republic of Ireland.

The defeat of the old Gaelic order in the Nine Years War, 1594-1603 and the escape of the most prominent Gaelic Lords of Ulster in 'the Flight of the Earls' in 1607 from Lough Swilly, County Donegal were ultimately responsible for the settlement of many English and Scottish families in the northern counties of Ireland.

Movement of Scottish settlers in a private enterprise colonisation of Counties Antrim and Down began in earnest from 1605 when Sir Hugh Montgomery and Sir James Hamilton acquired title to large estates in north Down and Sir Randall MacDonnell, 1st Earl of Antrim, to large tracts of land in north Antrim. In 1609 the Earl of Salisbury suggested to James I a more formal, deliberate plantation of English and Scottish colonists in Counties Armagh, Cavan, Donegal, Fermanagh, Londonderry (then known as Coleraine) and Tyrone.

These settlers came to Ulster, by and large, in three waves: with the granting of the initial leases in the period 1605 to 1625; after 1652 and Cromwell's crushing of the Irish rebellion; and, finally, in the fifteen years after 1690 and the Glorious Revolution. Famine in Scotland (which reduced Scotland's population by 10-15%) from 1695-1700, together with landlords in Ulster actively seeking new tenants, resulted in a massive influx of Scottish settlers to Ulster in the 1690s.

By the end of the 17th century a self-sustaining settlement of English and Scottish colonists had established itself in Ulster. One estimate of British population of Ulster is 40,000 by 1640, 120,000 by 1670 and 270,000 by 1712. It is also estimated that by 1715, when Scottish migration to Ulster had virtually stopped, the Presbyterian population of Ulster, i.e. of essentially Scottish origin, stood at 200,000.

Londonderry, Coleraine, Carrickfergus, Belfast and Donaghadee were the main ports of entry into the province of Ulster for 17th century British settlers with the Lagan, Bann and the Foyle valleys acting as the major arteries along which the colonists travelled into the interior.

Substantial numbers of Scottish families entered Ulster through Derry and settled in the Foyle Valley which includes much of the fertile lands of Counties Donegal, Londonderry and Tyrone. The lands along the Firth of Clyde in Ayrshire; the Clyde Valley; Wigtown, Kirkcudbright and Dumfries in Galloway; and the Border Lands of Berwick, Peebles, Selkirk and Roxburgh were home to many of these Scottish settlers.

Pacification of the riding families of the Borders, also known as Border Reivers (who, through raids on horseback, lived by cattle stealing and kidnapping), which began in earnest from 1603 with the Union of the Crowns of England and Scotland; religious conflict in southwest Scotland in the 1670s which culminated in the severe persecution of Presbyterians, in the so-called

'Killing Times', in Ayrshire in the period 1684-1688; and four successive harvest failures, in the 1690s, resulting in famine throughout both the Highlands and the Lowlands, all generated successive waves of Scottish emigrants to the Foyle Valley.

English settlers, mostly drawn from the northern counties of Cheshire, Cumberland, Lancashire, Northumberland, Yorkshire and Westmorland tended to favour settlement along the Lagan Valley in the east of the Province.

The London Companies who planted much of County Derry found it hard to hold their ill-prepared and ill-suited English settlers. The Companies, therefore, looked to the durable Scottish farmers to tenant their estates. As a consequence, surnames of Scottish origin dominate the Plantation names of the Derry area and owing to the Highland influence many of these names have Gaelic origins.

Anglicisation and Surname Variants

Inconsistency in spelling of surnames is well known to those who have conducted research into their Irish family history. You will find that in the context of Irish historical records there are many spelling variations of the same name.

From the 17th century Gaelic surnames were anglicised. Some names were translated into English while others were changed to a similar-sounding English name. This process of anglicisation, together with illiteracy, gave rise to numerous spelling variations of the same name. Uniformity in spelling surnames is really a phenomenon of the 20th century. The clergy, in entering relevant details on say a baptism register, often had to write down names based on pronunciation as many people could not write down or spell their name. Names of Gaelic origin were, furthermore, disguised by the widespread discarding of the prefixes of Mac, Mc and O in the 18th century.

Anglicisation will, in many cases, obscure the true origin of a surname. For example, Smith may be an English name or the anglicisation of the Gaelic McGowan (meaning son of Smith). Many surnames in the Derry area, such as Clarke, Green, Mitchell and Rodgers, could have originated independently in England, Scotland or Ireland; only detailed family history will confirm the actual origin.

Thus, in conducting family history research you should be aware of the possibility of different spellings of the same surname. Although, today in Derry, Doherty is the conventional way of spelling Gaelic *O Dochartaigh*, you will find that in the context of Irish historical records there are many spelling variations of this name; such as Daugherty, Docherty, Dogherty, Dougherty, Docherty, O Dochartaigh, O'Doagharty, O'Dogherty, and O'Doherty.

20th Century Settlers

More recent arrivals from outside of Ireland and Britain have also contributed a small but interesting collection of surnames in the Derry area.

A strong Italian community, with surnames such as Battisti, Caffola, Cassoni, Centra, Corrieri, Del Pinto, Fiorentini, Forte, Macari, Vaccaro and Yannarelli, was well-established in the city when General Balbo and his Italian squadron of 24 seaplanes landed on the Foyle, on 2 July 1933, on their transatlantic journey from Rome to Chicago. The Italian community in Derry tended to set up in either the restaurant or ice cream trade.

There were two separate influxes of Jewish migrants to Derry. The first wave, with surnames including Bernstein, Blogh, Frieslander, Gordon, Lazarus, Morris, Philman, Robinson, Spain and Welskey, arrived around the 1890s-1900s and they were Russian and Polish Jews fleeing from the pogroms there. Many of them didn't come directly to Derry but did so after stopping off in other cities such as Glasgow and Manchester. Around 50-60 families settled in Derry and they had their own synagogue with a rabbi in Kennedy Place. A number of these Jewish families anglicised their names, most were engaged in shop-keeping although a number of them were pedlars, taking goods from door to door.

The second influx of Jews arrived here in the 1930s, around 1937/1938, just before Hitler started instigating his anti-Jewish policies. These Jews were different from the Russian/Polish Jews. Most came from Austria and many of them were quite wealthy. They set up businesses. They included Madame Beck, a milliner; Fred Szilagyi who started a shirt factory, and Ludovic Schenkel who arrived here from Vienna in 1938 with just 10 shillings and started a business making canvas bags in Bigger's Stores on Foyle Street. Derry's Jewish population was at its peak in 1940 when the *Jewish Year Book* records that there were 109 Jewish Residents in Derry city.

A thriving Indian Community, represented by surnames such as Chada, Singh, Siripurapu, Vig and Vij, was first established in the city in the 1930s, most of whom originate from the Punjab in northern India. In the early years, new Indian arrivals to the city stayed at 4 Simpson's Brae in the Waterside district of Derry until they got themselves established. *Derry Almanac and Directory* of 1939 records Mohabat Rai Vij as the occupier of 4 Simpson's Brae in 1939.

United States Navy personnel stationed in the one-time Communications Base have married local girls and made their roots here.

More recent immigrants to the area are the Chinese with origins in Hong Kong's rural villages.

Sources

Standard reference books were used to compile this dictionary. They include:

Irish Families by Edward MacLysaght
More Irish Families by Edward MacLysaght
The Surnames of Ireland by Edward MacLysaght
The Book of Ulster Surnames by Robert Bell
A Dictionary of British Surnames by P.H. Reaney
A Dictionary of Surnames by Patrick Hanks and Flavia Hodges
The Penguin Dictionary of Surnames by Basil Cottle
The Concise Oxford Dictionary of English Place-Names by Eilert Ekwall
The Surnames of Scotland by George F. Black
The Clans and Tartans of Scotland by Robert Bain
Welsh Surnames by T.J. Morgan and Prys Morgan

These reference books should be consulted by those who wish to delve deeper into the subject of surname origins.

The Top 40 Surnames of Derry/Londonderry
Source: Foyle Community Directory of 1989

Surname	Rank	Number of Entries in Directory
Doherty	1	469
McLaughlin	2	246
Gallagher	3	170
Kelly	4	142
Moore	5	125
Coyle	6	116
Harkin	7	114
Bradley	8	110
Campbell	9	110
McDaid	10	105
Lynch	11	96
Brown	12	91
O'Donnell	13	91
Hamilton	14	89
Smith	15	84
Hegarty	16	72
Quigley	17	69
Duffy	18	68
Barr	19	65
Thompson	20	65
McCallion	21	64
Carlin	22	63
McCloskey	23	60
Mullan/Mullen/Mullin	24	60
Wilson	25	60
McDermott	26	59
Boyle	27	58
Morrison	28	58
O'Kane	29	55
O'Doherty	30	54
Cassidy	31	53
McGowan	32	53
McCafferty	33	52
Millar/Miller	34	51
Devine	35	50
O'Neill	36	50
Simpson	37	49
Stewart	38	49
Donaghy/Donaghey	39	48
McCauley	40	48

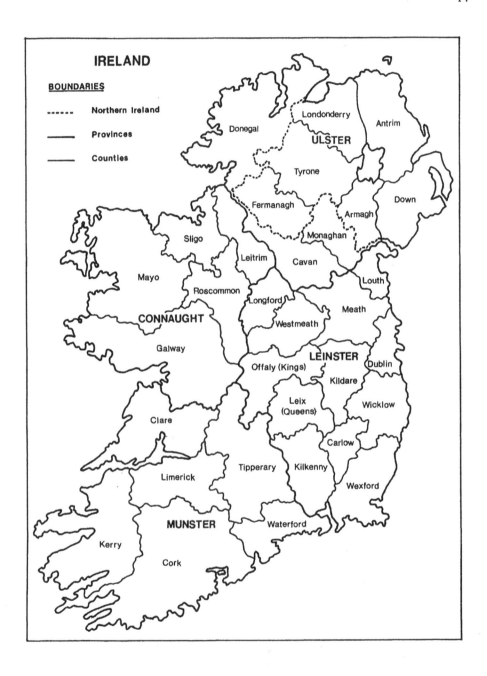

IRELAND

BOUNDARIES

- - - - - Northern Ireland

———— Provinces

———— Counties

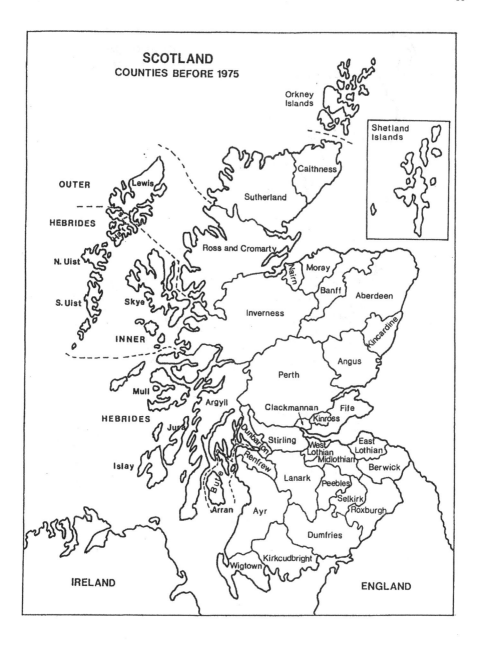

SCOTLAND
COUNTIES BEFORE 1975

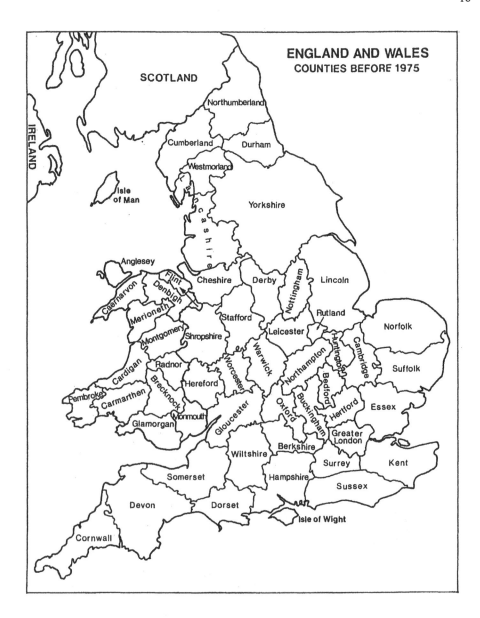

ENGLAND AND WALES
COUNTIES BEFORE 1975

The Top 300 Surnames of Derry/Londonderry

Surname	Rank	Origins
Adair	190	*Scottish.* Derived from the Old English personal name of Edgar. The name was first recorded in the province of Galloway in southwest Scotland in the 13th century and, by the 14th century, the Edgars of Dumfriesshire were being recorded as Adair.
Adams	254	Can be of *English, Scottish* or *Irish* origin. In England and Scotland it was derived from the popular medieval christian name of Adam. In the Highlands of Scotland, Adams was a sept of Clan Gordon while in Ireland a number of distinct septs with origins in Counties Armagh, Cavan and Monaghan anglicised their name to Adams.
Allen	112	*English.* Derived from the popular Norman name Alan. *Scots Gaelic.* There were several distinct septs of Allens but most stem from Clans MacFarlane and MacDonald.
Anderson	119	*Scottish.* Meaning son of Andrew this name can be found throughout Scotland. The Andersons were a sept of Clan Donald on Islay and Kintyre and of Clan Chattan in northeast Scotland as well as being one of the smaller riding clans of the Scottish Borders.
Arbuckle	191	*Scottish.* Derived from a place name in Lanarkshire, meaning height of the shepherd.
Armstrong	75	*Scottish.* Acquiring lands in the Scottish Borders in the 14th century the Armstrongs became one of the most powerful of the riding clans. At the height of their power they could muster an army of 3,000 men. In the 16th century neither the English nor Scottish crowns could control their forays for cattle and loot.
Austin	273	*English* and *Scottish.* Derived from the personal name Augustine, meaning venerable, this surname was first recorded in Ireland in the 14th century. Around 1230 an Augustinian monastery was established in Derry on the site where St. Augustine's church stands today.
Ball	236	*English* and *Scottish.* This name has various origins including: a nickname for a short, overweight person; a local name for someone who lived by a rounded hill; and an Old Norse personal name. It was introduced into Ireland from the 12th century.
Barr	19	*Scottish.* Derived from various place names in southwest Scotland, meaning height or hill. *English.* The name has various origins including: a local name for someone who lived by a gateway or barrier; an occupational name for a maker of bars; and a nickname for a tall, thin person.

Surname	Rank	Origins
Beattie	274	*Scottish.* Derived from the personal name Bate, which was in turn derived from the medieval personal name Bartholomew. The Beatties became well known in Galloway and the Borders of Scotland where they were one of the smaller riding clans.
Begley	142	*Irish.* A County Donegal sept, a branch of which migrated to County Kerry in the 15th century as galloglasses (mercenary soldiers). The parish name of Tullaghobegley in west Donegal commemorates their former association with this area.
Bell	120	*English* and *Scottish.* Variously derived from an occupational name for a bell ringer, from a nickname meaning beautiful or from a local name for someone who lived near a bell. It was a common name in the Scottish Borders where they were one of the riding clans. Bell was also common in the Isles where they were a branch of Clan MacMillan.
Black	96	*English.* Derived from a nickname which can mean both 'black' or 'dark' and 'white' or 'pale' depending on the original language root. *Scots Gaelic.* Septs of this name belonged to Clans Lamont, MacGregor and MacLean. Many members of Clan Lamont and Clan MacGregor adopted this colour name on their proscription by the Crown in the 17th century. Most Ulster Blacks are of this origin.
Bonner	121	*Irish.* This County Donegal sept, especially prominent around Ballybofey, bears one of the oldest surnames in Ireland which was first recorded in 1095. In Derry, Bonners will largely be of this origin. This surname, however, also originated in England where it derived from a nickname meaning gentle or courteous. A few settlers may have brought this name to Ulster.
Boyd	97	*Scots Gaelic.* Derived either from the place name, the Isle of Bute, or from a nickname meaning 'yellow'. As well as becoming well-established in Ayrshire and Edinburgh the Boyds were a sept of Clan Stewart.
Boyle	27	*Irish.* A County Donegal sept, with their heartland at Cloghaneely, who alongside the O'Dohertys and the O'Donnells controlled northwest Donegal in medieval times. *English* and *Scottish.* Derived from Beauville in France a family of this name accompanied William the Conqueror to England in 1066. A branch also settled in Scotland, becoming well established in Ayrshire. The Boyles of Limavady who settled there in 1660 are of this stock.

Surname	Rank	Origins
Bradley	8	*Irish*. The territory of this sept was on the borders of Counties Derry, Donegal and Tyrone. In Derry, Bradley will largely be of this origin. *Scots Gaelic*. A branch of the Irish Bradleys settled in the Western Highlands where one of its members became Abbot of Iona in the 12th century. *Lowland Scottish*. Derived from the place name of Braidlie in Roxburghshire.
Brady	163	*Irish*. This powerful sept at one time ruled a large territory to the east of Cavan town in the ancient Kingdom of Breffny.
Brennan	275	*Irish*. Several septs of the name originated in Counties Galway, Kerry, Roscommon and Westmeath but most in Ulster will be descended from a County Fermanagh sept who trace their descent from Eoghan, son of the 5th century High King of Ireland, Niall of the Nine Hostages.
Breslin	55	*Irish*. This Donegal sept ruled territory centred on Inniskeel on the Fanad peninsula. They later migrated to Fermanagh where they became hereditary lawyers to the Maguires. Breslin and O'Morison, another County Donegal sept, also anglicised their names to Bryson.
Brolly	276	*Irish*. Derived from an Old Irish personal name, Brollach. Originating in County Derry, in lands between the Rivers Foyle and Roe, this sept, who trace their descent from Eoghan, son of the 5th century High King of Ireland, Niall of the Nine Hostages, also had its name anglicised to Brawley.
Brown	12	*English* and *Lowland Scottish*. Derived in most cases as a nickname for someone who was 'brown-haired' or 'brown-skinned'. An Anglo-Norman family of this name settled in Ireland in the 12th century. *Scots Gaelic*. At least two septs, one meaning son of the judge and the other meaning son of the brown lad, had their names anglicised to Brown. On their outlawing by the Crown in the 17th century one of the names adopted by members of Clan Lamont was Brown.
Browne	104	This spelling of Brown tends to be more common in the South of Ireland. *English* and *Lowland Scottish*. Derived in most cases as a nickname for someone who was 'brown-haired' or 'brown-skinned'. An Anglo-Norman family of this name settled in Ireland in the 12th century. *Scots Gaelic*. At least two septs, one meaning son of the judge and the other meaning son of the brown lad, had their names anglicised to Brown. On their outlawing by the Crown in the 17th century one of the names adopted by members of Clan Lamont was Brown.
Buchanan	171	*Scottish*. This clan takes its name from the lands of Buchanan in Stirlingshire. It was founded by a branch of the O'Kanes of Derry who settled in Argyll in 1016.

Surname	Rank	Origins
Burke	89	*English.* Derived from a local name for a fortification. In Ireland the Burkes, who came to be regarded as a great gaelic sept, trace their descent from William de Burgo, a Norman knight from Suffolk who invaded Ireland with Henry II in 1171 and received the earldom of Ulster.
Burns	98	*Scots Gaelic.* Originally a Clan Campbell sept who took their name from Burnhouse in Argyllshire. In addition Scottish McBurney and Irish O'Byrne were anglicised to Burns.
Cairns	151	*Scottish.* Derived from the lands of Cairns in Midlothian the name became well established in Galloway, a region in southwest Scotland, from the early 15th century.
Caldwell	152	Can be of *English, Scottish* or *Irish* origin. In England and Scotland it derived from a number of place names meaning cold spring or stream. In Ireland at least two septs, namely Horish of Tyrone and Cullivan of Cavan, anglicised their names to Caldwell.
Callaghan	237	*Irish.* There were two septs of this name, of which the more powerful one was based in County Cork. The majority of Ulster Callaghans, however, descend from the Kelaghan sept whose stronghold was outside Fivemiletown in County Tyrone.
Callan	277	*Irish.* It may be a variant of McCallion. The McCallions were the galloglasses (mercenary soldiers) of Clan Campbell of Argyll who came to Donegal in the 16th century to fight for the O'Donnells. It can also be a contracted from of O'Callan, a County Monaghan sept. Some may have Scots Gaelic origins as a variant of McAllan, with septs of this name belonging to Clans MacFarlane and MacDonald.
Campbell	9	*Scots Gaelic.* Derived from a nickname meaning crooked mouth the Campbells of Argyll grew in power through the 17th century at the expense of the MacDonalds, Lords of the Isles. Most Ulster Campbells are of this connection. The galloglasses or mercenary soldiers of Clan Campbell settled in Donegal from the 15th century. *Irish.* The County Tyrone sept of McCawell, whose name meant son of the battle chief, was anglicised as Campbell. At the height of their power in the 12th century, from their base at Clogher, they controlled a large portion of County Tyrone and had penetrated deep into County Fermanagh.
Canning	72	*English.* Most County Derry Cannings descend from the Cannings of Garvagh who came to Ulster in 1615 from Warwickshire as agents to the estate of the London Company of Ironmongers. Canning was derived from the Wiltshire place name of Cannings. Occasionally the County Donegal sept name of Cannon became Canning.

Surname	Rank	Origins
Carlin	22	*Irish*. Tracing their descent from Eoghan, son of the 5th century High King of Ireland, Niall of the Nine Hostages, and originating in the Laggan district of County Donegal the Carlins or O'Carolans were the leading sept of Clan Dermot who were very powerful in the neighbourhood of Derry during the 11th and 12th centuries. Although eventually overrun by the O'Kanes the parish name of Clondermot or Glendermot is a reminder of their former prominence and the townland name of Lismacarrol, meaning the fort of the sons of Carroll, as a former base.
Carruthers	278	*Scottish*. Derived from the lands of Carruthers in Dumfriesshire it was first recorded as a surname in the early 14th century. In 1587 they were recorded as one of the unruly clans of the Scottish Borders.
Casey	122	*Irish*. There were at least seven distinct septs of the name. The County Fermanagh sept of O'Casey were hereditary tenants of the church lands of Devenish. Other septs of the name originated in Counties Cork, Dublin, Limerick, Mayo, Monaghan and Roscommon.
Cassidy	31	*Irish*. A County Fermanagh sept who were hereditary physicians to the Maguires. The stronghold of the chief of the Cassidys was at Ballycassidy, in the parish of Trory, just to the north of the town of Enniskillen.
Cavanagh/ Kavanagh	192	*Irish*. This sept, with origins in County Wexford, were of the same stock as the McMurroughs, the late 12th century kings of Leinster. The McCavanas of east Tyrone and the McKevenys of south Antrim sometimes anglicised their name to Cavanagh or Kavanagh
Chada	279	Arriving in Derry in 1930 the Chadas were the first Indians to settle in Ireland. The original bearer of the name came to Derry via Kenya where he was a self-taught mechanic. He arrived in Derry on board a ship which had sailed from Mombasa via Marseilles. Settling in Derry the Chadas built up a thriving footwear and drapery business which by 1957 was employing 25 people. By 1957 the Indian community in the city stood at 50.
Chambers	172	*English* and *Scottish*. Derived from an occupational name for a chamber attendant it was first recorded as a surname in Scotland in the 13th century.

Surname	Rank	Origins
Clarke	69	Can be of *English*, *Scottish* or *Irish* origin. In England and Lowland Scotland Clark derived as an occupational name for a clerk or cleric while in Ireland and Highland Scotland Clark was a further anglicisation of O'Clery and McCleery. In Scotland, there were McCleery septs, meaning son of the cleric, attached to Clans Campbell, Cameron, Macpherson and Mackintosh. In Ireland, a branch of the O'Haras of Sligo, who settled in County Antrim, were known as McCleary; and the County Galway sept of O'Clery established themselves in Derry and Donegal from the 13th century. They became regarded as a literary sept through their compilation of the famous "Annals of the Kingdom of Ireland by the Four Masters" in Donegal town.
Clifford	143	*English*. Derived from various place names meaning ford at a cliff or slope. At the end of the 16th century a family of this name settled in County Sligo. *Irish*. The County Kerry sept name of Cluvane was widely changed to Clifford.
Colhoun	73	*Scottish*. This clan takes its name from the lands of Colquhoun in Dunbartonshire which they acquired in the 13th century. In the 16th and 17th centuries they were involved in a bitter feud with the McGregors.
Collins	123	*English*. Derived from the christian name Colin which in turn was derived from the popular medieval name Nicholas. *Irish*. Cullen, with origins in Counties Donegal and Monaghan, was sometimes further anglicised to Collins.
Connor	238	*Irish*. A variant of O'Connor. There were at least six distinct septs of this name, including the O'Connors of Roscommon and Sligo who were High Kings of Ireland in the 12th century. The O'Connors of Derry, whose territory was overrun by the O'Kanes in the 12th century, trace their lineage to Cian, King of Munster in the 3rd century.
Cooke	153	*English*. Derived from an occupational name for a cook. *Scots Gaelic*. As an abbreviated form of McCooke they were a Clan Donald sept of Kintyre and Aran.
Coyle	6	*Irish*. Meaning son of the servant of Comgall this sept established itself in Mevagh parish, County Donegal. An early form of the name was McIlhoyle. Furthermore Coyle has become confused with McCool.
Craig	76	*Scottish*. Derived from a local name for someone who lived near a crag or rock. By the 15th century this surname was common throughout Edinburgh and the Lowlands of Scotland.

Surname	Rank	Origins
Crossan	133	*Irish.* Originally McCrossan there were two distinct septs of the name. The County Tyrone sept was the more numerous and it provided two Bishops of Raphoe in the 14th century. The Crossans of County Leix were hereditary poets to the O'Mores and O'Connors.
Crumley	280	*Irish.* This sept originated in Counties Derry and Donegal. In some cases it may be a variant of Crumlish. The Crumlish sept, whose name originally meant descendant of the squint-eyed man, originated in County Donegal.
Cunningham	83	*Scottish.* This clan takes its name from the district of Cunningham in Ayrshire. During the 17th century Plantation of Ulster many Cunninghams settled in Donegal. *Irish.* Cunningham was the adopted anglicisation of a number of septs such as McCunnigan of Donegal and Conaghan of Derry.
Curran	42	*Irish.* There were several distinct septs of this name. In Galway they were a branch of the O'Maddens while in Waterford and Tipperary the Currans were a big sept by the 17th century. The name is numerous in Derry and Strabane today because a Curran sept also originated in Donegal.
Curry	207	*Irish.* There were two distinct septs of this name; one originating in County Clare, the other in Westmeath. *Scots Gaelic.* Septs of this name, meaning son of Murdock, were branches of Clan Donald and Clan MacPherson. It may also be a variant of Corry. The south Derry name of Corr and the Fermanagh sept of McCorry, who were a branch of the Maguires, were also known as Corry, and, in the neighbourhood of Derry, the O'Corrys were one of the septs of Clan Dermot, with the parish name of Clondermot or Glendermot being a reminder of their former prominence. In Scotland, Corry was derived from the Dumfriesshire place name of Corrie, and the McCorrys were a sept of Clan Macquarrie of Mull.
Daly	173	*Irish.* This sept originated in County Westmeath but later migrated to County Cavan where they became hereditary poets to the O'Reillys.
Davis	220	*Welsh.* Derived from Welsh name Dafydd, meaning son of Davy. *Scottish.* A sept of Clan Davidson. Meaning son of David, Clan Davidson was originally part of Clan Chattan confederation with lands in Perthshire and Inverness-shire. *Irish.* A variant of McDaid, meaning son of David, the County Donegal sept who take their name from the O'Doherty chief of that name who died in 1208. At the turn of the 20th century Davis was being used interchangeably, in parts of Derry and Tyrone, with both Davidson and McDaid.

Surname	Rank	Origins
Deehan	208	*Irish.* In a few cases this sept with origins in County Derry have had their name changed to Dickson.
Deeney	113	*Irish.* Originating in County Donegal this sept was strongly represented in the priesthood in the Diocese of Raphoe from the 15th century.
Deery	99	*Irish.* Originating in County Derry this sept were hereditary stewards of the church lands in Derry city itself. The County Donegal sept name of O'Derry has to a large extent been absorbed into Deery.
Devine	35	*Irish.* Tracing their descent from the 10th century King of the ancient Kingdom of Oriel the Devines were a leading County Fermanagh sept until their power was checked by the O'Neills and the Maguires in the 15th century.
Devlin	124	*Irish.* This County Tyrone sept, who ruled over territory on the west shore of Lough Neagh, trace their descent from Eoghan, son of the 5th century High King of Ireland, Niall of the Nine Hostages. The chief of the sept was hereditary swordbearer to O'Neill.
Dillon	239	*English.* Derived from the Germanic personal name Dillo it was introduced into England by the Normans in the 11th century and then to Ireland in the 12th century. The Dillons acquired vast territories in County Westmeath and, in time, became regarded as a great gaelic sept. In some cases the County Limerick sept name of Dillane was made Dillon.
Doherty	1	*Irish.* This name, a variant of O'Doherty, is by far the most popular name in Derry. This County Donegal sept, which originated in Raphoe but settled in Inishowen from the 14th century, can trace their lineage to Conall Gulban, son of the 5th century High King of Ireland, Niall of the Nine Hostages. They ruled Inishowen until the arrival of an English army at Derry in 1600. An O'Doherty-led rebellion, which included the ransacking of Derry in 1608, helped pave the way for the Plantation of Ulster.
Donaghy/ Donaghey	39	*Irish.* This anglicisation of McDonagh established itself in Counties Derry and Tyrone. Stemming from the personal name Donagh, meaning brown warrior, McDonagh septs originated in County Sligo as a branch of the O'Flahertys and in County Cork as a branch of the McCarthys.
Donnelly	46	*Irish.* As a branch of the O'Neills this sept can trace its lineage to Eoghan, son of the 5th century High King of Ireland, Niall of the Nine Hostages. Originating in County Donegal they later migrated to Tyrone where their chief was hereditary marshal in O'Neill's army.
Doran	100	*Irish.* Originally one of the 'Seven Septs of Leix' this sept established itself in Counties Armagh and Down.

Surname	Rank	Origins
Downey	81	*Irish.* There were two distinct septs of the name. In County Galway they were a branch of the O'Maddens while in County Down Muldowney was shortened to Downey. *Scots Gaelic.* Derived either from the lands of Duny or Downie in Angus or as a shortened form of McIldownie which meant son of the lord's servant.
Duddy	47	*Irish.* This distinct sept, whose name in gaelic was the same as that of O'Dowd who ruled over extensive territory in Mayo and Sligo, originated in County Derry and anglicised their name to Duddy.
Duffy	18	*Irish.* Two distinct septs of this name originated in Ulster, one in Monaghan who were based at Clontibret, the other in Donegal where they were hereditary tenants of the church lands of Templecrone. *Scots Gaelic.* A sept of Clan MacFie who trace their descent from Kenneth McAlpine, the 9th century King of Scots. Meaning 'son of the black one of peace' this clan's home was on the island of Colonsay in the Hebrides.
Dunlop	154	*Scottish.* Derived from the lands of Dunlop in Ayrshire, meaning muddy hill, it was first recorded as a surname in the mid-13th century. Dunlop became established in both Kintyre and north Antrim owing to 17th century plantations in both areas.
Dunn/ Dunne	84	*Irish.* This powerful sept originated in County Leix where they became lords of Iregan and noted opponents of English incursions in the mid-16th century. *Scottish.* They were one of the smaller riding clans on the English side of the Scottish Borders.
Edwards	281	*English* and *Scottish.* Meaning son of Edward it was derived from the given name made popular by two Kings of England, namely the 10th century Edward the Martyr and the 11th century Edward the Confessor.
Elliott	221	*Scottish.* Derived from the Old English personal name Elwald the Elliotts were one of the great riding clans of the Scottish Borders. During the 17th century Plantation of Ulster they tended to settle in Fermanagh.
Farren	255	*Irish.* A sept of this name originated in the Inishowen peninsula in County Donegal. In addition the County Armagh sept name of Fearon tended to become Farron in Donegal.
Faulkner	174	*English* and *Scottish.* Derived from the occupational name for a trainer or keeper of falcons it was recorded as a surname in Scotland from 1200. Some Faulkners in Ireland may descend from one Nicholas Taylor, the 13th century 'Falconer' to Henry III.

Surname	Rank	Origins
Ferguson	64	*Scots Gaelic*. Clan Ferguson who claim descent from the 2nd century Irish King, Conn of the Hundred Battles, first settled on Kintyre. Since Fergus was a popular christian name the surname Ferguson spread all over Scotland, including the province of Galloway which was the homeland of many Ulster Fergusons.
Ferris	240	*Irish*. The County Donegal sept of O'Ferry and the County Mayo sept of O'Fergus sometimes became anglicised as Ferris. *Scots Gaelic*. A branch of Clan Ferguson. Clan Ferguson who claim descent from the 2nd century Irish King, Conn of the Hundred Battles, first settled on Kintyre.
Ferry	144	*Irish*. This County Donegal sept, who were followers of the McSweeneys, can trace their descent from Conal Gulban, son of the 5th century High King of Ireland, Niall of the Nine Hostages.
Finlay	222	*Scots Gaelic*. The Finlays were a sept of Clan Farquharson and their name originally meant son of the fair hero. The name was also anglicised to McKinley.
Fitzpatrick	256	*Irish*. Meaning son of the devotee of Patrick this County Kilkenny sept assumed the Norman prefix Fitz, meaning son, in the 16th century. The name was in some cases anglicised to Kilpatrick. Derived from a number of place names meaning church of Patrick the Kilpatricks were a sept of Scottish Clan Colquhoun.
Fleming	114	*English* and *Scottish*. Meaning a native of Flanders many Flemings settled in Scotland and Wales in the 12th century. They first came to Ireland from Wales in the same century as the Norman invaders and they acquired considerable lands in County Meath. Many more, however, came from Scotland with the 17th century Plantation of Ulster.
Foster	209	*English* and *Scottish*. The most likely origin of this surname is as an abbreviated form of Forester, which derived from the occupational name for a forest keeper. The Fosters were one of the great riding clans of the Scottish Borders.
Fox	210	*Irish*. A number of distinct septs, including the McAtinney sept of south Tyrone and Armagh, meaning son of the fox, anglicised their name to Fox. *English* and *Scottish*. Derived from a nickname referring to 'slyness'.
Frazer	282	*Scottish*. Derived from the place name of La Fresiliere in Anjou in France this surname was first recorded in Scotland in the 12th century. As Clan Frazer they acquired the lands of Lovat which stretched along the eastern shores of Lough Ness.

Surname	Rank	Origins
Friel	90	*Irish*. This County Donegal sept can trace their lineage to Eoghan, a brother of St. Columkille who, by tradition, founded the monastic settlement at Derry in 546. The Friels held the hereditary right of inaugurating O'Donnell as Lord of Tirconnell.
Gallagher	3	*Irish*. This is the third most common surname in Derry. This County Donegal sept can trace its lineage to Conal Gulban, son of the 5th century High King of Ireland, Niall of the Nine Hostages. Controlling extensive territories stretching from Raphoe to Ballyshannon they were the chief marshals in the army of O'Donnell, Prince of Tirconnell.
Gamble	283	*English*. This name which frequently appeared in the 11th century Domesday Book was derived from an Old Norse personal name.
Gibbons	257	*Irish*. The Norman name of Fitzgibbon, established in Counties Limerick and Mayo by 12th century Anglo-Norman invaders, and the County Mayo sept name of McGibbon, who were a branch of the Burkes, have been made Gibbons. *English*. Derived from a Germanic personal name.
Gibson	193	*Scottish*. Stemming from the personal name Gilbert there were septs of this name attached to Clans Buchanan, Cameron and Campbell.
Gill	211	A variant of McGill. *Scots Gaelic*. Meaning son of the stranger or Lowlander McGill was a common surname in Galloway in southwest Scotland. McGills from Jura settled in Antrim from the 14th century. *Irish*. Many Irish septs adopted the prefix Mac Gille which meant son of the follower (e.g. MacGilpatrick meant son of the follower of Patrick). At a later date, in many cases, the prefix (i.e. McGill) became the surname itself.
Gillen	223	*Irish*. A variant of McGillen. A County Derry sept which can trace its lineage to Eoghan, son of the 5th century High King of Ireland, Niall of the Nine Hostages. Gillen, in many cases, has become indistinguishable from McGilligan, another County Derry sept who, in the early 17th century, were one of the chief septs under the O'Kanes. Their territory is known to us today as Magilligan.
Gillespie	48	*Irish* and *Scots Gaelic*. This name originally meant son of the servant of the Bishop. In Ireland Gillespie originated as a County Down sept which settled, at an early period, in County Donegal where they became hereditary tenants of the church lands of Kilcar. In Scotland the Gillespies were a sept of Clan MacPherson. By translation the name also became Bishop.

Surname	Rank	Origins
Glenn	134	*Irish* or *Scots Gaelic*. Derived from various local names referring to someone who lived in a valley. In Scotland the name was also derived from the lands of Glen in Peebleshire.
Gorman	258	*Irish*. Originating in County Leix near the town of Carlow this sept settled in west Clare and Monaghan at the time of the Norman invasion. The Gormans of County Clare were hereditary marshals to the O'Briens. Denoting descent from Brian Boru, High King of Ireland in the early 11th century, the O'Briens controlled a great part of the Province of Munster and vied with the O'Neills of Ulster and O'Connors of Connaught for the High Kingship of all Ireland.
Gormley	125	*Irish*. Tracing their descent from Eoghan, son of the 5th century High King of Ireland, Niall of the Nine Hostages, this sept settled in County Tyrone, to the east of Strabane, in the 14th century when they were pushed out of their homeland in Raphoe, County Donegal by the O'Donnells.
Graham	175	*Scottish*. A Norman family of this name, derived from the Lincolnshire place name of Grantham, settled in Scotland in the early 12th century and acquired lands in Midlothian. They also settled in the Scottish Borders where they became one of the most powerful riding clans. In some cases Gormley was anglicised to Graham.
Grant	91	*Scottish*. This clan claims descent from Kenneth MacAlpine, the 9th century King of Scotland. In the 13th century they appear as Sheriffs of Inverness and from then up to the 17th century they asserted considerable influence in the Northeast of Scotland.
Green	135	*Irish*. A number of distinct septs, including the County Derry sept of McGlashan, anglicised their name to Green. *English*. Derived from a local name for someone who lived near a village green.
Griffin/ Griffen	259	*English* and *Welsh*. Derived either as a nickname for a 'fierce person' or as a variant of the Welsh personal name Griffith. A Welsh family of Griffen did settle in Ireland soon after the 12th century Anglo-Norman invasion. *Irish*. Most Griffins in Ireland were originally O'Griffy who originated as a sept in northwest Clare.

Surname	Rank	Origins
Hamilton	14	*Scottish.* Derived from the Yorkshire place name of Hambleton, meaning crooked hill, this surname was introduced to Scotland in the 13th century by a Norman family from Leicestershire. In the 14th century the Hamiltons were granted the lands of Cadzow in Lanarkshire by Robert the Bruce. Hamilton is a name very much associated with the Scottish 'undertakers' or landowners who were granted large estates in Counties Armagh, Fermanagh and Tyrone at the time of the 17th century Plantation of Ulster.
Hanna	284	*Scots Gaelic.* A powerful sept in the Province of Galloway in southwest Scotland who were forced to submit to their Norman conquerors led by Edward Bruce in 1308.
Hargan	194	*Irish.* This variant of the County Cork sept name of Horgan is largely confined to Ulster. Harrigan is also a recorded variant of Hargan.
Harkin	7	*Irish.* This County Donegal sept, with their homeland in the Inishowen peninsula, were hereditary tenants of the church lands of Clonca, near Malin Head.
Harper	285	*Scots Gaelic.* Derived from an occupational name referring to a harp player. The harper was a hereditary office in the households of most clan chiefs. Anglicised to Harper the original form of the name was McWhirter. The Harpers or McWhirters were a sept of Clan Buchanan and the name was most common in Argyllshire and Stirlingshire.
Harrigan	80	*Irish.* As well as being a recorded variant of Hargan there was a County Leix sept who anglicised their name to Harrigan.
Harvey	155	Can be of *English, Scottish* or *Irish* origin. In Ireland the County Donegal sept name of Harrihy was anglicised to Harvey. In England and Scotland the name was derived from an Old French name, meaning battle worthy, which was introduced to Britain with the Norman invaders in the 11th century.
Haslett/ Hazlett	224	*English.* Derived from a local name for someone who lived by a hazel copse. Although originally an English name Haslett and its variants such as Hazlett, Heslitt and Heazley are now chiefly found in Northern Ireland.
Hasson	115	*Irish.* Recorded as Hassan, Hassen, Hasson and Hessan in historical documents this surname originated in County Derry.
Healy/ Healey	145	*Irish.* Two septs of this name originated independently in south Cork and on the western shore of Lough Arrow in County Sligo. In Cork the name was also known as Healihy.
Heaney	136	*Irish.* The principal sept of this name were chiefs of Fermanagh before the Maguires took over in 1202. Another sept of the name were hereditary tenants of the church lands of Banagher in County Derry.

Surname	Rank	Origins
Hegarty	16	*Irish*. Originating in south Derry this sept can trace its descent from Eoghan, son of the 5th century High King of Ireland, Niall of the Nine Hostages. By the 17th century they had established themselves in Inishowen, County Donegal and in County Derry, west of the River Roe. The Hegartys were sub-lords to the O'Neills.
Henderson	137	*Scottish*. Derived from the popular Norman forename Henry the Hendersons were variously a sept of Clan Gunn in Caithness; a clan, with 8th century origins in Glencoe in Argyllshire who, in the 14th century, became the bodyguards and hereditary pipers to the McDonalds of Glencoe; and one of the lesser riding clans of the Scottish Borders.
Henry	195	Can be of *English*, *Scottish* or *Irish* origin. In England it derived from the Germanic personal name Henry which was introduced there by the Normans. In Scotland the Henrys of Argyll and Bute were originally McKendricks. Meaning son of Henry, the McKendricks were a sept of Clan MacNaughton. In Ireland the north Antrim/Derry sept of McHenry, who were a branch of the O'Kanes, and the County Derry sept of O'Henery were further anglicised to Henry.
Herron	212	*Irish*. Two septs, one originating in County Armagh and the other in Donegal, anglicised their names to Harran, Herron, Heran or Heron. The County Armagh sept name of McElheron, meaning son of the devotee of Ciaran, was in some cases shortened to Heron. *Scots Gaelic*. On the Isle of Bute there was a sept of McElheran attached to Clan Donald while in the Scottish Borders the Herons were one of the lesser riding clans. In England, Heron derived as a nickname for a thin man with long legs.
Hetherington	176	*English*. Derived from a Northumberland place name meaning settlement of the dwellers on the heath. The name was established in County Leix in the 16th century although it is now mainly found in County Tyrone.
Higgins	241	*Irish*. Claiming descent from the 5th High King of Ireland, Niall of the Nine Hostages, this sept originated in the Midlands of Ireland but spread westward into Mayo and Sligo. Some will be of English descent where the name originally meant little Richard.
Holmes	225	*Scots Gaelic*. A number of septs, whose name meant son of Thomas, anglicised their name to Holmes and to McComb. Septs of this name were attached to Clans Campbell, Mackintosh, MacTavish and MacThomas. Some may take their name from the lands of Holmes in Ayrshire. *English*. Derived from a local name for someone who lived on fen land.

Surname	Rank	Origins
Houston	164	*Scottish*. Meaning Hugh's place many Houstons descend from a Norman family who settled in Lanarkshire in the 12th century. Their lands came to be called Huston and, at a later date, they adopted their estate's name as their surname. In some cases, in Donegal, McHugh was anglicised to Huston and Houston.
Hughes	242	*English*. Meaning son of Hugh this popular personal name was introduced to Britain by the Normans in the 11th century. *Irish*. At least five septs in Ulster, whose names meant descendant of Hugh, anglicised their name to Hughes. The Ulster septs of this name originated in west Armagh, south Donegal, south Down, south Monaghan and north Tyrone. Indeed, there were at least 12 distinct Irish septs whose names, meaning descendant of Hugh, were variously anglicised to O'Hea in southwest Cork, Hughes in Ulster and Hayes in the remainder of the country.
Hunter	196	*English* and *Scottish*. Derived from an occupational name for a huntsman. It was first introduced to Scotland in the early 12th century by the Normans and the name became very common in Ayrshire. The Hunters were also one of the lesser riding clans of the Scottish Borders.
Hutchinson	243	*Scots Gaelic*. Meaning son of Hutcheon, which in turn meant little Hugh, this sept, with origins in the Isle of Skye, trace their descent from Hugh, son of Alexander McDonald, Lord of the Isles. This name is also anglicised as Hutcheson and Hutchison.
Hutton	126	*English* and *Scottish*. Derived from a great number of place names meaning ridge settlement it was recorded as a surname in Scotland in Lanarkshire from the mid-13th century.
Hyndman	260	*English* and *Scottish*. Derived from an occupational name for a servant this surname is now chiefly found in Northern Ireland. Hyndman was recorded in Renfrewshire, Scotland from the 16th century.
Irvine	286	*Scottish*. Derived from the parish of Irving in Dumfriesshire the Irvines became one of the more troublesome riding clans of the Scottish Borders. During the Plantation of Ulster many Irvines settled in Fermanagh where they gave their name to Irvinestown. The name has, however, become confused with Irwin.
Irwin	197	*Scottish*. Derived from the Old English personal name of Irwyn. During the 17th century plantation most Irwins who settled in Ulster came from Dumfriesshire. Although a distinct name, Irwin is often confused with Irvine.

Surname	Rank	Origins
Jackson	92	*English* and *Scottish*. Meaning son of Jack this surname is very common in all parts of the British Isles. In Ulster it is found mainly in Counties Antrim and Armagh.
Johnston	44	*Scottish*. Strictly speaking Johnson and Johnston are two distinct surnames; the former meaning son of John and the latter John's town. The two names, however, are now indistinguishable one from the other. The Johnstones were one of the great riding clans of the Scottish Borders who settled in Dumfriesshire in the lands of Johnstone in the 12th century. During the Plantation of Ulster many of them settled in Fermanagh. Furthermore septs of Clan Gunn in Caithness and of Clan Donald in Glencoe anglicised their name to Johnson and Johnston. In Ireland a number of septs including McKeown and McShane anglicised their name to both Johnson and Johnston.
Jones	244	*Welsh*. Meaning son of John this extremely popular Welsh name is especially associated with Counties Antrim and Armagh where English settlement dominated during the 17th century Plantation of Ulster.
Kane	198	*Irish*. A variant of O'Kane. The sept of O'Kane or O'Cahan can trace their lineage to Eoghan, son of the 5th century High King of Ireland, Niall of the Nine Hostages. Originating in the Laggan district of County Donegal the O'Kanes, who were the leading sept of Clan Connor, settled in the Dungiven area, County Derry from the 10th century. By the 12th century they had established themselves in County Derry from the Foyle to Bann rivers and they had gained the privilege of inaugurating the chief of the O'Neills.
Kearney	185	*Irish*. Tracing their descent from Eoghan, son of the 5th century High King of Ireland, Niall of the Nine Hostages, the Kearneys were a branch of the O'Hanlons of Armagh.
Keenan	146	*Irish*. A County Fermanagh sept who acted as historians to the Maguires and who were hereditary stewards of the church lands of Cleenish.
Kelly	4	*Irish*. At least seven distinct septs of the name established themselves in Ireland, the most powerful of which ruled over a territory which included east Galway and south Roscommon. In Ulster, a Kelly sept, claiming descent from Colla, the 4th century King of Ulster, was based in south Derry. Kelly was known as a surname in Scotland long before the 19th century immigration really established the name there; there was a Kelly sept attached to Clan Donald.

Surname	Rank	Origins
Kennedy	186	*Irish*. This sept takes its name from the father of Brian Boru, the early 11th century High King of Ireland. Originating in east Clare they later settled in north Tipperary where they became Lords of Ormond from the 11th century to the 16th century. In the early 17th century a branch of the sept settled in County Antrim. *Scottish*. Originating in Ayrshire in the 12th century the Kennedys settled in Lochaber in Inverness-shire where they were a sept of Clan Cameron.
Kerr	105	*Scottish*. As one of the great riding clans they settled in Roxburgh in the Scottish Borders in the 14th century. The majority of Ulster Kerrs are of this origin. Kerr, however, has become confused with Carr. A number of Ulster septs, such as Kilcarr of Donegal and Carry of Armagh, anglicised their name to Carr.
Kerrigan	261	*Irish*. This sept originated in County Mayo. A branch later migrated to the Stranorlar area in County Donegal and, by the mid-17th century, the name was also established in County Armagh.
Keys	66	*English and Scottish*. This name has various origins including: an occupational name for a key maker; a Welsh personal name, i.e. Kay; and a local name for someone who lived near a quay. In Northern Ireland, however, most Keys will originally have been McKee. *Scots Gaelic* McKee is another anglicisation of Clan Mackay, which meant son of Hugh. In some instances McKee may be a variant of *Irish* McHugh.
Kilgore	199	*Scottish*. Derived from the Fifeshire place name of Kilgour meaning goat wood this name was common in Fifeshire and Aberdeenshire. In Ireland the northwest Ulster sept name of Kilgar was anglicised to Kilgore.
King	177	*English* and *Scottish*. As a nickname King was widely adopted as a surname in England and Scotland. In Perthshire a sept of Clan MacGregor anglicised their name to King. Some Ulster septs such as McAree of Monaghan and McGinn of Tyrone anglicised their name to King.
Lafferty	287	*Irish*. Originating in County Donegal, the chiefs of this sept were Lords of Aileach before they were driven from their homeland in the 13th century and settled near Ardstraw in County Tyrone. Lafferty can also be another form of Laverty. *Scots Gaelic*. A Laverty sept attached to Clan Donald were hereditary heralds to the Lords of the Isles. Originating in Kintyre the Lavertys were later based on Islay.
Leonard	262	*Irish*. Various Ulster septs adopted this English personal name when anglicising their name such as McAlinion of Fermanagh and O'Lunney of Donegal.

Surname	Rank	Origins
Lindsay	226	*Scottish.* This clan traces its descent from one Baldric de Lindsay, a Norman who held extensive lands in Angus in the 12th century. In Ulster, Lynch and Lynn were in some cases further anglicised to Lindsay.
Logan	227	*Scottish.* This clan, also known as McLennan, trace their origins to one Logan who, in the 14th century, acquired lands in Ross and Cromarty. Logan was originally derived from several places of that name, especially in Ayrshire, meaning little hollow. A Norman family of the name settled in Carrickfergus, County Antrim in the 12th century. Furthermore, the County Galway sept name of Lohan was sometimes anglicised to Logan.
Logue	51	*Irish.* A County Galway sept, whose name originally meant descendant of the devotee of Maodhog, who migrated at an early date to Derry and Donegal. The name is now rare outside these two counties. Mulvogue was another form of the anglicisation of this name. In Donegal Logue was in some cases changed to Molloy, an important sept in counties Offaly and Roscommon.
Long	93	Can be of *English*, *Scottish* or *Irish* origin. In England and Scotland it derived as a nickname meaning 'tall' while in Ireland the County Armagh sept name of Longan was anglicised to Long.
Loughrey	228	*Irish.* Mainly found in Ulster, and originally meaning descendant of the early riser, this surname has, in some instances, become confused with the ecclesiastical sept names of Early in County Cavan and Loughran in County Armagh.
Lynch	11	*Irish.* Derived from the personal name meaning mariner there were several septs of the name including one based in north Antrim and Derry. In medieval Galway Lynchs of Anglo-Norman origin were all-powerful. In England Lynch derived as a local name for someone who lived by a hill.
Lynn	288	*Irish.* As the Ulster form of Flynn, derived from the gaelic personal name Flann, this sept once ruled territory to the east of Lough Neagh in south Antrim. *Scottish.* Lynn was also known in Ayrshire and Wigtownshire from the 13th century where it was derived from the name of a waterfall near the ancient Castle of Lin in Ayrshire.
Lyttle/ Little	74	Can be of *English*, *Scottish* or *Irish* origin. In England it derived as a nickname meaning 'small' and in Scotland the Littles were one of the riding clans of the Scottish Borders. In Ireland many members of the County Monaghan sept of Beggan anglicised their name to Little.

Surname	Rank	Origins
Mackey	293	*Scots Gaelic*. A variant of Mackay. Meaning son of Hugh, Clan Mackay came to prominence in Sutherland in the 13th century. The Mackays were also septs of Clan Davidson in Inverness-shire and of Clan Donald in Kintyre. Confusion arises as this name has acquired in the process of anglicisation a great number of variants. This name was also anglicised as Mackie, McCay, McCoy, McKay, McKee and McKie. The first Mackays or McCays to settle in Ireland, also known as McCoy, were Clan Donald galloglass (mercenary soldiers), fighting for the McDonnells of the Glens of Antrim.
Magee	101	*Scots Gaelic*. Meaning son of Hugh this name was first recorded in Dumfries in the 13th century. They were connected to the Clan Donald sept of Mackay. *Irish*. Septs of this name, meaning son of Hugh, were based in: Islandmagee, County Antrim; Kilmacrenan, County Donegal; and in Fermanagh where they were a branch of the Maguires.
Maguire	229	*Irish*. This County Fermanagh sept established itself at Lisnaskea around 1200. By 1300 the Maguires were rulers of all Fermanagh. In a few cases the name may derive from Scotland where MacGuire was a sept of Clan MacQuarrie on the island of Ulva.
Mahon	267	*Irish*. A Variant of McMahon. There were two distinct septs of this name. In Ulster the McMahons ruled County Monaghan from the decline of the O'Carrolls in the early 13th century. In west Clare the McMahons were a branch of the O'Briens, Kings of Munster.
Mallet	179	*English*. A Norman family of the name accompanied William the Conqueror to England in 1066. A Huguenot family, called Malet or Mallet, settled in Kent, in the late 18th century, and in County Cork. There are five known origins of this name with the most interesting being that of a nickname for 'a fearsome warrior.'
Martin	59	Can be of *English, Scottish* or *Irish* origin. In Ireland it may be an abbreviation of the County Tyrone sept name of McMartin and of the County Fermanagh sept name of McGilmartin. In England the personal name Martin became, at an early date, a popular surname while in Scotland septs of the name were attached to Clan Cameron in Inverness-shire and to Clan Donald in Skye.
McAdams	263	*Irish*. Two Ulster septs, namely McCaw of County Cavan and McCadden of County Armagh, anglicised their name to McAdam. *Scots Gaelic*. First recorded in 1160, McAdams was a sept of Clan MacGregor in Ayrshire.

Surname	Rank	Origins
McAllister	127	*Scots Gaelic*. Meaning son of Alasdair, the gaelic form of Alexander, this clan is the earliest offshoot of the great Clan Donald. Descended from Alasdair Mor, the younger son of Donald of the Isles, this clan's territory was principally in Kintyre. They came to Ulster as galloglasses (mercenary soldiers) to the McDonnells of Antrim.
McBride	60	*Irish*. Meaning son of the devotee of Brigid this County Donegal sept, who were based at Gweedore, were hereditary tenants of the church lands of Raymunterdoney. *Scots Gaelic*. This sept of Clan Donald, who were based on Arran Island, trace their descent from Gillebride, father of Somerled, the 12th century Lord of Argyll.
McCafferty	33	*Irish*. Meaning son of the horse rider this sept originated in County Donegal as a branch of the O'Donnells. The name has become confused with McCaffrey, a sept which traces its decent from Donn Carrach Maguire, King of Fermanagh, who died in 1302.
McCallion	21	*Scots Gaelic*. Meaning son of Colin the McCallions were the galloglasses (mercenary soldiers) of Clan Campbell of Argyll. In the 16th century they came to Donegal to fight for the O'Donnells.
McCandless	289	*Irish*. This Ulster name, derived from the Old Irish personal name of Cuindleas, was also recorded as McAndles and McCanliss.
McCann	156	*Irish*. This County Armagh sept were Lords of Clanbrassil on the southern shores of Lough Neagh. The McCanns have been recorded there since 1155. Prior to this the O'Garveys ruled this territory.
McCarron	77	*Irish*. This County Donegal sept can trace their lineage to Eoghan, son of the 5th century High King of Ireland, Niall of the Nine Hostages. It is also possible that a sept of this name originated along the banks of the Foyle and later migrated to Monaghan.
McCarter	165	*Scots Gaelic*. A variant of McArthur. Claiming to be the older branch of Clan Campbell the McArthur clan acquired extensive territory in Argyll in the early 14th century in recognition of their support of Robert the Bruce who, at Bannockburn in 1314, secured Scotland's independence from England.
McCartney	138	*Scots Gaelic*. Meaning son of Art this sept was a branch of Clan Mackintosh. The name was recorded in Ayrshire and Galloway from the early 16th century and in northeast Ulster from the mid-17th century. It is believed that Scottish McCartneys were originally Irish McCartans, a County Down sept who were sub-lords to the McGuinnesses.

Surname	Rank	Origins
McCaul	245	*Irish.* The County Tyrone sept of McCawell, a leading sept in that county in the 12th century who can trace their descent from Eoghan, son of the 5th century High King of Ireland, Niall of the Nine Hostages; and the County Monaghan sept of McColla, who were a branch of the McMahons, anglicised their names to McCaul. *Scots Gaelic.* Meaning son of Cathal, and anglicised as McAll, McCall and McCaul, this name was common in Ayrshire and Dumfriesshire. The McCauls originated as branches of both the McAuleys and McDonalds.
McCauley	40	*Scots Gaelic.* There were two septs of this name; on Lewis in the Hebrides they were a sept of Clan MacLeod while in Dunbartonshire the McAuleys were a branch of Clan MacGregor. A branch of the latter sept accompanied the McDonalds to the Glens of Antrim in the early 16th century. *Irish.* A County Fermanagh sept who trace their descent from Donn Carrach Maguire, the first Maguire King of Fermanagh, who died in 1302.
McCay	94	*Scots Gaelic.* A variant of Mackay. Meaning son of Hugh, Clan Mackay came to prominence in Sutherland in the 13th century. The Mackays were also septs of Clan Davidson in Inverness-shire and of Clan Donald in Kintyre. Confusion arises as this name has acquired in the process of anglicisation a great number of variants. This name was also anglicised as Mackey, Mackie, McCoy, McKay, McKee and McKie. The first Mackays or McCays to settle in Ireland, also known as McCoy, were Clan Donald galloglass (mercenary soldiers), fighting for the McDonnells of the Glens of Antrim.
McClay	95	*Scots Gaelic.* Meaning son of the physician, and numerous in Easter and Wester Ross and in Argyll, the McClays were a sept of Clan Stewart of Appin. They frequently anglicised their name to Livingstone and Lee.
McClean	290	*Scots Gaelic.* Meaning son of the servant of John, Clan Maclean, which traces its descent from the 13th century Gillean of the Battle-axe, acquired extensive territories in Argyllshire, including the island of Mull. They came to Ulster in the 16th century as galloglasses (mercenary soldiers) to both the O'Donnells and the O'Neills. This surname is frequently spelt as McLean.
McClelland	85	*Scots Gaelic.* Meaning son of the devotee of Fillan this name was common in the Province of Galloway from the 14th century.

Surname	Rank	Origins
McClintock	147	*Scots Gaelic.* Meaning son of the devotee of Fintan, a 7th century Irish saint who was a disciple of Saint Columba, this name was recorded in Argyllshire and Dunbartonshire from the early 16th century. McClintock is most numerous in Counties Antrim and Derry. In some cases the name was anglicised to Lindsay.
McCloskey	23	*Irish.* This County Derry sept is very much associated with the Dungiven area. They were a branch of the O'Kanes, tracing their descent from the 12th century Bloskey O'Cahan.
McColgan	102	*Irish.* In the 11th and 12th centuries the McColgans were the most powerful sept in the Derry area. They were a branch of Clan Dermot and they were hereditary tenants of the church lands of Donaghmore in County Donegal. From the 13th century onwards the influence of the O'Kanes was to increase at the expense of the McColgans.
McConnell	139	*Scots Gaelic.* The McConnells were a sept of the McDonnells, the Glens of Antrim branch of Clan Donald. By the mid-16th century Scottish Clan Donald held extensive territory in the Glens of Antrim at the expense of the McQuillans
McConomy	213	*Irish.* A County Derry/Tyrone sept whose name meant son of the hound of Meath. The name was further anglicised to Conway. At the turn of the 20th century Conway was still being used interchangeably with McConomy in Counties Derry and Tyrone.
McCool	106	*Irish.* Meaning son of the servant of Comgall this sept was based in Raphoe, County Donegal.
McCorkell	107	*Scots Gaelic.* Tracing their name from an Old Norse personal name, meaning Thor's kettle or cauldron, which became Thirkill in England, the McCorkells were a sept of Clan Gunn. In Ireland this name is mainly confined to Counties Derry and Donegal.
McCormick	108	*Scots Gaelic.* Meaning son of Cormac the McCormicks were a prominent sept of Clan Maclean on the island of Mull. *Irish.* A number of septs, including a branch of the Maguires, adopted this name.
McCourt	128	*Irish.* This name is most numerous in Counties Antrim, Armagh and Monaghan. This is to be expected as a sept of this name originated in south Armagh. In County Monaghan the name was further anglicised to Courtney.

Surname	Rank	Origins
McCready	148	*Irish*. A County Donegal sept who were hereditary tenants of the church lands of Tullaghobegley, a parish consisting of rugged land between the Rosses and Bloody Foreland in west Donegal. Descended from this sept was 'Father Donogh MacReidy, of Coleraine, Dean of Derry, who in 1608 suffered martyrdom by being pulled asunder by four horses'. *Scots Gaelic*. Recorded as MacRedie in Ayrshire and as MacReadie and MacCreadie in Galloway in southwest Scotland.
McCullagh	291	*Irish*. Meaning son of the hound of Ulster this name originated east of the River Bann in the ancient Kingdom of Dal Riata. Under increasing pressure from the expanding dynasties claiming descent from the 5th century High King of Ireland, Niall of the Nine Hostages, the peoples of east Ulster began to settle in Scotland. By the 6th century they had founded a colony in Argyll, and the term Scot originally referred to these Gaelic colonists from eastern Ulster. Today the surname McCullagh is most numerous in Counties Antrim, Down and Tyrone. *Scots Gaelic*. McCullagh was recorded in Wigtown in the late 13th century. In Oban in Argyllshire the McCullaghs were a sept of Clan MacDougall, tracing their descent from Dugald, son of Somerled, the 12th century Lord of Argyll who expelled the Norsemen from the Western Isles. The name is also spelt as McCulloch, McCullogh, McCullough and McCully.
McDaid	10	*Irish*. This County Donegal sept was a branch of the Dohertys. Meaning son of David they take their name from the O'Doherty chief of that name who died in 1208. In a few cases McDaid may be a variant of the Scottish clan name Davidson.
McDermott	26	*Irish*. This County Roscommon sept was a branch of the O'Connors, Kings of Connaught before the Norman invasions of the 12th century. A few may be of Scottish origin as in Perthshire there was a Clan Campbell sept of this name.
McDevitt	187	*Irish*. This County Donegal sept was a branch of the Dohertys. Meaning son of David they take their name from the O'Doherty chief of that name who died in 1208. This name was also anglicised as McDaid.

Surname	Rank	Origins
McDonald	264	*Scots Gaelic.* In historical times Clan Donald trace their lineage to 12th century Somerled, Lord of Argyll, who expelled the Norsemen from the Western Isles. Folklore traces their descent back to the semi-legendary Irish King, Conn of the Hundred Battles. They take their name from Donald, a grandson of Somerled. As Lord of the Isles with territory stretching from the Outer Hebrides to Kintyre the McDonalds became the most powerful clan in Scotland. The Lordship was broken up by the Scottish Crown in 1493. Throughout the 17th century they vied with the Campbells for the position of 'Headship of the Gael'. In Ireland McDonalds were recorded as galloglasses (mercenary soldiers) in Tyrone from the end of the 13th century. By the mid-16th century the McDonnells, a branch of Clan Donald, held extensive territory in the Glens of Antrim at the expense of the McQuillans.
McDowell	129	*Scots Gaelic.* Meaning son of the black foreigner the McDowells descend from Duggal, the son of Somerled who was the founder of Clan Donald. Clan Donald trace their lineage to 12th century Somerled, Lord of Argyll, who expelled the Norsemen from the Western Isles.
McElhinney	130	*Irish.* Meaning son of the devotee of Canice, a sixth century Irish missionary saint, this County Derry sept can trace their lineage to Eoghan, son of the 5th century High King of Ireland, Niall of the Nine Hostages.
McFadden	70	*Irish.* Meaning son of Patrick this sept originated in west Donegal. *Scots Gaelic.* This sept of Clan Maclean was first recorded in Kintyre in 1304. On the Isle of Mull they were known as the race of the goldsmiths.
McFarland	200	*Irish.* Meaning son of Bartholomew this sept of noted poets, based in south Armagh, was first recorded in the 15th century. *Scots Gaelic.* Tracing their descent from the ancient Earls of Lennox, Clan McFarlane inhabited lands on the western shores of Loch Lomond in Dunbartonshire. Owing to their warlike tendencies the clan was proscribed and dispossessed of its lands in the late 16th century.
McFeely	166	*Irish.* This name originated in the Derry/Donegal area. By 1831 the name was well established in County Derry to the west of the River Roe. McFeely/McFeeley is quite distinct from the County Cork sept name of O'Feely or Fehilly.
McGarrigle	265	*Irish.* Mainly associated with County Donegal, McGarrigle is a variant of the Cavan/Leitrim name McGirl. This name was also anglicised to Cargill in Donegal.
McGeady	157	*Irish.* Originating in northwest Donegal this surname was first recorded in Derry city in the mid-1820s in the registers of Long Tower Chapel.

Surname	Rank	Origins
McGeehan	266	*Irish*. Originating in County Donegal, in the Glenties area, McGeehan is now indistinguishable from McGahan which is associated with Counties Armagh, Monaghan and Tyrone.
McGill	246	*Scots Gaelic*. Meaning son of the stranger or Lowlander this surname was common in Galloway in southwest Scotland. McGills from Jura settled in Antrim from the 14th century. *Irish*. Many Irish septs adopted the prefix Mac Gille which meant son of the follower (e.g. MacGilpatrick meant son of the follower of Patrick). At a later date, in many cases, the prefix (i.e. McGill) became the surname itself.
McGilloway	54	*Irish*. Meaning son of the yellow-haired youth this sept originated in County Donegal. The name was also anglicised to McElwee, McIlwee and McKelvey.
McGinley	56	*Irish*. This County Donegal sept played an important part in church affairs in the Diocese of Raphoe. The name is often confused with McKinley. In Scotland McKinley septs belonged to Clans Buchanan, Farquharson, MacFarlane and Stewart of Appin.
McGlinchey	167	*Irish*. Originating in County Donegal, and also anglicising their name to McClinchy, this sept name is chiefly found today in Counties Derry, Donegal and Tyrone.
McGowan	32	*Irish*. Meaning son of the smith the most powerful sept of this name originated in County Cavan. Other septs of the name were also based at Inishmacsaint, County Donegal and at Clogher, County Tyrone. *Scots Gaelic*. As the maker of arms the smith was an important hereditary position in each clan. As a consequence the surname Smith was associated with most clans. This surname, more than any other, has suffered at the hands of anglicisation. Many Smiths in Ulster today were originally McGowan.
McGrory	178	*Irish*. Meaning son of Rory there were two septs of the name in Ulster. A County Derry sept were hereditary tenants of the church lands of Ballynascreen while in Fermanagh the McGrorys were a branch of the Maguires. *Scots Gaelic*. They were an important Clan Donald sept, some of whom came to Ulster as galloglasses (mercenary soldiers) in the early 14th century.

Surname	Rank	Origins
McGuinness	86	*Irish*. Meaning son of Angus this powerful sept, based at Rathfriland, controlled most of County Down as Lords of Iveagh from the 12th century until the 17th century Plantation of Ulster. In some cases McGuinness is a variant of the Scottish clan name MacInnes. Also meaning son of Angus this clan traces its origins to the Irish Celts, known as Scots, from eastern Ulster who settled in Argyll. The Scots were crossing the narrow sea from Ireland in 4th and 5th centuries and had established a power base in Argyll by the 6th century.
McIntyre	58	*Scots Gaelic*. Meaning son of the carpenter this clan settled at Lorn in Argyllshire from the Hebrides around 1400. A branch of the family were hereditary pipers to the chiefs of Clan Menzie. The name has become much confused with McAteer, a County Armagh sept, whose name has also been changed to McIntyre. In the Glens of Antrim McIntyre was frequently anglicised to Wright while in Fermanagh McAteer was sometimes anglicised to Wright.
McIvor	140	*Irish*. This County Derry sept derived its name from the Norse personal name Ivar. *Scots Gaelic*. In addition to Clan McIver which acquired lands in Argyll in the 13th century there were septs of the name belonging to Clans Campbell, MacKenzie and Robertson.
McKeegan	292	*Irish*. The sept names of Keegan or McKeegan originated in two widely separated areas, namely in Counties Dublin/Wicklow and in Counties Leitrim/Roscommon. It is claimed that the McKeegans of North Uist in the Western Isles of Scotland arrived there from Ireland around 1600.
McKeever	103	A variant of McIvor. *Irish*. This County Derry sept derived its name from the Norse personal name Ivar. *Scots Gaelic*. In addition to Clan McIver which acquired lands in Argyll in the 13th century there were septs of the name belonging to Clans Campbell, MacKenzie and Robertson. Some McKeevers may descend from a branch of the McMahons of County Monaghan.
McKenna	230	*Irish*. This County Meath sept settled at an early date in County Monaghan where they became Lords of Truagh. A few may be of Scottish origin as the name was recorded in Galloway in southwest Scotland in the 17th century.
McKinney	61	*Irish*. There was a County Tyrone sept of this name. In some cases McKinney was a variant of McKenna. *Scots Gaelic*. Another name for Clan MacKinnon which claimed descent from Kenneth MacAlpine, the 9th century King of Scotland. The clan held lands in Mull and Skye. In Ulster some Scottish MacKenzies adopted the name McKinney.

Surname	Rank	Origins
McKnight	247	*Scots Gaelic*. A sept of Clan MacNaughton. Members of this clan settled in the Glens of Antrim, in the early 17th century, alongside the MacDonnells. By the mid-16th century the McDonnells, a branch of Clan Donald, held extensive territory in the Glens of Antrim at the expense of the McQuillans.
McLaughlin	2	*Irish*. The second most popular name in Derry. Derived from the Norse personal name Lachlann this County Donegal sept can trace its lineage to Eoghan, son of the 5th century High King of Ireland, Niall of the Nine Hostages. In the 12th century the McLaughlins, from their Inishowen homeland, were High Kings of Ireland and patrons of the monastic settlement in Derry. From the mid-13th century the O'Neills of Tyrone ousted the McLaughlins as the leading power in Ulster. Some may be of Scottish descent from Clan MacLachlan of Argyll.
McMahon	294	*Irish*. There were two distinct septs of this name. In Ulster the McMahons ruled County Monaghan from the decline of the O'Carrolls in the early 13th century. In west Clare the McMahons were a branch of the O'Briens, Kings of Munster.
McMenamin	82	*Irish*. This County Donegal sept were followers of the O'Donnells. Concentrated around Letterkenny and Ballybofey the name is largely confined to Donegal and West Tyrone.
McMonagle	65	*Irish*. This sept name is very much associated with County Donegal where it is now one of the most common surnames. In a few instances the prefex Mac was dropped.
McMorris	295	*Irish*. It can be a gaelicised form of Fitzmaurice, meaning son of Maurice, the Norman family who became Lords of Lixnaw in County Kerry. In County Mayo another Norman family called Prendergast adopted McMorris as their surname.
McMullan	231	*Scots Gaelic*. A variant of McMillan. Meaning son of the bald one, which referred to a religious tonsure, Clan McMillan acquired the lands of Knapdale in Argyllshire in the 14th century. In Ulster this name frequently became McMullan as it was adopted by Scottish planters as a means to distinguish themselves from Irish O'Mullan. Understandably there can be confusion between McMullan, O'Mullan and Mullan.
McNeill	296	*Scots Gaelic*. Claiming descent from Niall, twenty-first in descent from the 5th century High King of Ireland, Niall of the Nine Hostages, this clan settled in Barra in the Outer Hebrides in 1049. In the 14th century McNeills came to Ulster as galloglasses (mercenary soldiers) and settled in Counties Derry and Antrim. They were Lords of Clandeboy in County Antrim, along with the McQuillans, for a while in the 15th century before submitting to the O'Neills in 1471.

Surname	Rank	Origins
McNulty	232	*Irish*. Meaning son of the Ulsterman this sept originated in south Donegal. One of the names assumed by Dunleavys when they settled in Donegal was McNulty. Dunleavy was an ancient Irish family who were driven from County Down by the Normans in the 12th century and settled in Donegal.
McShane	201	*Irish*. Meaning son of John this sept, based in northeast Tyrone, was a branch of the O'Neills. The name was frequently anglicised to Johnson.
Meehan	202	*Irish*. Septs of this name were based in Counties Clare/Galway and in Leitrim. The latter sept, a branch of the McCarthys, settled in Leitrim in the 11th century. They later spread to Fermanagh where they became hereditary tenants of the church lands of Devenish.
Meenan	158	*Irish*. This sept originated in County Donegal in the district between Rathmullan and Ramelton.
Melaugh	214	*Irish*. Meaning devotee of Saint Aodhog this name is chiefly found today in the Derry area. In 1831 census, as Malaugh, the name was to be found in Glendermot parish.
Mellon	180	*Irish*. Tracing their descent from Eoghan, son of the 5th century High King of Ireland, Niall of the Nine Hostages, this sept originated to the south of the Sperrin Mountains in north Tyrone. The name has become confused with Mullan.
Millar/Miller	34	*English* and *Scottish*. As every manor or estate had its miller this occupational surname sprang up all over England and Scotland. Millar is usually regarded as the Scottish spelling of the name.
Mitchell	49	Can be of *English*, *Scottish* or *Irish* origin. Derived from the Hebrew personal name Michael, and in a few cases from a nickname meaning 'big', Mitchell became very numerous throughout England and Scotland. In Northeast Scotland the Mitchells were a sept of Clan Innes. Furthermore the Highland Scottish name of McMichael, septs of Clan Stewart of Appin and Clan Stewart of Galloway, was frequently anglicised to Mitchell. In Ireland, and in County Donegal especially, the County Roscommon sept name of Mulvihill was anglicised to Mitchell.
Molloy	159	*Irish*. Tracing their descent from the 5th century High King of Ireland, Niall of the Nine Hostages, the Molloys were an important sept in County Offaly. A branch later settled in County Roscommon. Molloy has also been recorded as a variant of the County Donegal name of Logue.
Monaghan	215	*Irish*. Meaning descendant of the monk the main sept of this name originated in County Roscommon. Monaghans in the Northwest, however, will trace their descent to the north Fermanagh sept of the name.

Surname	Rank	Origins
Montgomery	216	*Scottish*. Tracing their descent from Roger de Montgomery, Regent of Normandy, who accompanied William the Conqueror to England in 1066 this clan acquired lands in Renfrewshire in the 12th century. The various offshoots of the Montgomery families on the Ayrshire coast had established, by the early part of the 17th century, trading connections with Ulster.
Mooney	149	*Irish*. There were several distinct septs of the name, including a branch in County Donegal who were hereditary tenants of the church lands at Ardara.
Moore	5	Can be of *English, Scottish* or *Irish* origin. In England and Scotland the name derived from the personal name More, meaning Moor (i.e. the Muslim people of Northwest Africa) or from a local name for someone who lived on or near moorland. Moore became widespread as a surname throughout England and Scotland. In Scotland the name was also known as More and Muir. The Mores were a sept of Clan Leslie while the Muirs were a sept of Clan Campbell. In Ireland the O'Mores were the leading sept of the Seven Septs of Leix.
Moran	50	*Irish*. In the Province of Connaught there were four distinct septs of this name. In addition the County Fermanagh sept of McMorran has become Moran. Moran is also a recorded variant of Morahan which originated in Offaly and Leitrim. In some cases, as Morrin, it may be a Huguenot name. Many Huguenots fled to Ulster from France in the late 17th century in the face of persecution by Louis XIV.
Morrison	28	*Irish*. A County Donegal sept who were hereditary tenants of the church lands of Clonmany adopted this English name which meant son of Maurice. *Scots Gaelic*. Claiming descent from a Norse family shipwrecked on the Island of Lewis Clan Morrison, from their seat at Habost on the northern tip of the Isle of Lewis, became sub-lords to the MacLeods.
Morrow	268	*English*. Derived from a local name for someone who lived in a row of houses on moorland. *Irish*. A variant of McMorrow. Meaning son of the mariner, two distinct septs of McMorrow originated in Counties Fermanagh and Leitrim.
Mulhern	297	*Irish*. Originating in County Roscommon, where it was better known as Mulkerrin, a branch of this sept established itself in southwest Donegal.

Surname	Rank	Origins
Mullan/ Mullen/ Mullin	24	*Irish*. Meaning descendant of the bald one, which referred to a religious tonsure, and tracing their descent from the 5th century High King of Ireland, Niall of the Nine Hostages, the O'Mullan sept originated in the Laggan district of east Donegal. As a member of Clan Connor they accompanied the O'Kanes in their invasion and settlement of north Derry in the 12th century. Confusion is caused by the fact that the majority of Scottish Macmillans adopted the surname of McMullan, which, like O'Mullan, was frequently shortened to Mullan.
Murphy	62	*Irish*. Meaning descendant of sea warrior three major septs of the name originated in Counties Cork, Wexford and Roscommon. In the Northwest, however, many will be descended from the County Tyrone sept of McMurphy who trace their lineage to the 5th century High King of Ireland, Niall of the Nine Hostages. In Fermanagh a branch of the Maguires took the name Murphy.
Murray	45	*Scots Gaelic*. Taking their name from the northern province of Moray this clan acquired its territory in the 12th century from David I. *Irish*. Derived from a given name meaning mariner several septs of this name originated in Counties Cork, Down, Leitrim and Roscommon.
Nash	217	*English*. Derived from a local name, found in southern England, for someone who lived by an ash tree. An Anglo-Norman family of this name settled in County Kerry in the 13th century.
Neely	168	*Irish* and *Scots Gaelic*. This variant of McNeilly, meaning son of the poet, was particularly associated with County Antrim. McNeilly was established as a surname in Galloway, southwest Scotland by the 15th century. Furthermore, the County Galway sept name of Conneely was anglicised to Neely.
Nelis	248	*Irish*. A variant of McNelis. Originating as a sept in County Donegal their name is recorded as both McNelis and Nelis. McNelis tends to be peculiar to Donegal whereas Nelis is found in adjoining counties.
Nichol	116	*Irish*. A County Tyrone sept whose name was also anglicised as McNicholl and McNickle. *Scots Gaelic*. Clan MacNicol settled in Skye from the 14th century where they were sub-lords of Clan MacLeod. Owing to the further anglicisation of these names to Nicholls and Nicholson, which are forms that originated in England from the Latin name Nicholas, the exact origins of this name and its many variants can cause confusion.

Surname	Rank	Origins
Norris	150	*English* and *Scottish*. Derived from the Old French term Noreis, meaning Northerner. In the case of Ireland it originally referred to someone who had come from Scandinavia. As a surname it has been recorded in Ireland since the 13th century.
O'Brien	298	*Irish*. Denoting descent from Brian Boru, High King of Ireland in the early 11th century, this sept controlled a great part of the Province of Munster and vied with the O'Neills of Ulster and O'Connors of Connaught for the High Kingship of all Ireland.
O'Connell	181	*Irish*. This County Kerry sept was driven out of its homeland by the O'Donoghues in the 11th century.
O'Connor	131	*Irish*. There were at least six distinct septs of this name, including the O'Connors of Roscommon and Sligo who were High Kings of Ireland in the 12th century. The O'Connors of Derry, whose territory was overrun by the O'Kanes in the 12th century, trace their lineage to Cian, King of Munster in the 3rd century.
O'Doherty	30	*Irish*. This County Donegal sept, which originated in Raphoe but settled in Inishowen from the 14th century, can trace their lineage to Conall Gulban, son of the 5th century High King of Ireland, Niall of the Nine Hostages. They ruled Inishowen until the arrival of an English army at Derry in 1600. An O'Doherty-led rebellion, which included the ransacking of Derry in 1608, helped pave the way for the Plantation of Ulster. This name is also anglicised as Doherty.
O'Donnell	13	*Irish*. Taking their name from Domhnall, who died in 901, and tracing their descent from Conall Gulban, son of the 5th century High King of Ireland, Niall of the Nine Hostages, this sept, from their base around Kilmacrenan, County Donegal, rose in importance from the 13th century to the position of overlords of Donegal. The O'Donnells, alongside the O'Neills, led the Ulster Rebellion of 1594-1603 against English encroachment.
O'Hagan	63	*Irish*. This County Tyrone sept, with their base at Tullaghoge (near Cookstown), can trace their lineage to Eoghan, son of the 5th century High King of Ireland, Niall of the Nine Hostages. The O'Hagans were the hereditary custodians of Tullaghoge, the hill where the Ulster kings were inaugurated from the 11th century.
O'Hara	299	*Irish*. Originating in County Sligo a branch of this sept migrated to the Glens of Antrim in the 14th century.

Surname	Rank	Origins
O'Kane	29	*Irish*. The sept of O'Kane or O'Cahan can trace their lineage to Eoghan, son of the 5th century High King of Ireland, Niall of the Nine Hostages. Originating in the Laggan district of County Donegal the O'Kanes, who were the leading sept of Clan Connor, settled in the Dungiven area, County Derry from the 10th century. By the 12th century they had established themselves in County Derry from the Foyle to Bann rivers and they had gained the privilege of inaugurating the chief of the O'Neills.
Olphert	269	*Scottish*. This variant of Oliphant is chiefly found in Counties Antrim and Derry. The Oliphants of Norman origin, who settled in Northamptonshire, England in the late 11th century, acquired lands in Roxburghshire, Scotland in the 12th century. The Londonderry Port Book of 1612 to 1615 records the trading activity of Wibrant Olfert, a Dutch merchant, who made Derry his home in the very early years of the Plantation of Ulster; he was importing timber from Norway and exporting butter and oats.
O'Neill	36	*Irish*. Tracing their descent from Eoghan, son of the 5th century High King of Ireland, Niall of the Nine Hostages, this sept has one of the oldest surnames in Ireland. It has been in continuous use since King Domhnall in the 10th century adopted the name of his grandfather Niall, Black Knee. The senior branch of this sept, the O'Neills of Tyrone, were frequently High Kings of Ireland and in the 16th century they were the leaders of Gaelic resistance to English attempts to pacify Ireland. A junior branch established themselves in County Antrim in the 14th century and from their seat at Shane's Castle became known as the Clandeboy O'Neills.
O'Reilly	109	*Irish*. This powerful sept were chiefs of the ancient territory of Breffny which comprised Cavan and west Leitrim. At the height of their power in the middle ages their influence extended into Meath and Westmeath.
Orr	67	*Scottish*. Derived from the place name of Orr in Kirkcudbrightshire. It may also be an anglicisation of McIvor which may be of *Irish* or *Scots Gaelic* origin. The County Derry sept of McIvor derived its name from the Norse personal name Ivar. In Scotland, in addition to Clan McIver which acquired lands in Argyll in the 13th century there were septs of the name belonging to Clans Campbell, Robertson and MacKenzie.

Surname	Rank	Origins
Owens	249	*Irish*. A variant of both McKeown and O'Keown. Meaning son of John various septs adopted the surname McKeown. The major sept of the name was based in Sligo, but other known septs of McKeown originated in Counties Armagh and Fermanagh. The County Fermanagh sept of O'Keown were hereditary tenants of the church lands of Enniskillen. Some Owens may be of Welsh origin, simply meaning son of Owen.
Parke/ Park	203	*English* and *Scottish*. Derived from a local name for someone who lived in a park or enclosure of thinly wooded land. It can also be an abbreviation of Parker, derived from an occupational name for a park-keeper. In Scotland the surname was also derived from the lands of Park in Renfrewshire.
Parkhill	204	*Scottish*. Derived from the lands of Parkhill in Ayrshire it was recorded as a surname in Glasgow in 1605.
Patterson	205	*Scottish*. Meaning son of Patrick this name originated in the Lowlands of Scotland. In the Highlands the sept name of McPatrick, meaning son of the devotee of Patrick, was anglicised to Patterson. McFetridge, meaning son of Peter, of Galloway in southwest Scotland was often anglicised to Patterson. In Ireland the County Mayo sept name of McPadden was in some cases anglicised to Patterson.
Patton	233	Can be of *English*, *Scottish* or *Irish* origin. In England and Scotland Patton was variously derived from the personal name Patrick; from the place names of Patton in Shropshire and Westmorland; and from an occupational name for a clog maker. In Ireland the County Donegal sept of O'Pettane was anglicised to Patton.
Peoples	87	*Irish*. The east Donegal and west Derry sept name of Deeny was often mistranslated to Peoples. Both Peoples, also spelt Peebles, and Deeny are mainly found in the Raphoe area of Donegal. In England Peoples is a variant of Pepys.
Porter	57	*English* and *Scottish*. This occupational name can have three meanings, the most likely one being a doorkeeper. In the Middle Ages the office of porter was a very important one in both castle and monastery. In some cases Porter referred to a person who could be hired to carry baggage while in Scotland it had an additional meaning of ferryman. Porter was first recorded in Ireland in the 13th century.
Quigg	250	*Irish*. Originating as a sept in County Derry this name is chiefly found in this county. Quigg can also be a shortened form of Quigley. By the end of the 16th century a Quigley sept, which originated in County Mayo, had become dispersed with its main concentration located in Counties Derry and Donegal. A sept called Quigley also originated in the Inishowen peninsula, County Donegal.

Surname	Rank	Origins
Quigley	17	*Irish*. By the end of the 16th century this sept, which originated in County Mayo, had become dispersed with its main concentration located in Counties Derry and Donegal. A sept called Quigley also originated in the Inishowen peninsula, County Donegal.
Ramsey	110	*English* and *Scottish*. Derived from the place name Ramsay found in both Huntingdonshire and Essex. In Scotland Ramsays of Anglo-Norman origin acquired lands in Lothian in the 12th century. A century later they were landowners in Angus and as a clan they were beginning to figure prominently in the Border wars.
Rankin	218	*Scots Gaelic*. In Counties Derry and Donegal Rankins trace their descent from an Argyllshire sept of Clan Maclean. The McRankins of Glencoe, meaning son of Francis, were hereditary pipers to the Macleans. These Rankins were quite distinct from the Lowland Rankins, who were particularly common in Ayrshire, and who derived their surname from the personal name Randolph.
Reid	160	Can be of *English*, *Scottish* or *Irish* origin. In England and Scotland it was, in most cases, derived from a nickname meaning 'red', as in red hair or ruddy complexion. Some derived their name from various place names. In Scotland the Reids were one of the lesser riding clans of the Scottish Borders. Furthermore, the Highland septs of McRory and McInroy were anglicised as Reid. In Ireland the County Mayo sept of Mulderrig anglicised its name to Reid.
Robb	270	*Scottish*. Derived from the Old English personal name Robert this name was originally McRobb. In addition to being a sept of the Stewarts of Appin in Argyll, the McRobbs were septs of Clans Buchanan and MacFarlane.
Roberts	271	*English* and *Scottish*. Derived from the popular Old English personal name Robert this name, together with Robertson, became more common in Scotland than in England. In Perthshire, Clan Robertson took its name from their 15th century chief, Grizzled Robert. Clan Robertson was also known as Clan Donnachaidh. After the 1745 Jacobite Rising many Robertsons adopted the name Donachie which was further anglicised to Duncan. Members of Clan Robertson adopted this name after its 14th century chief, Fat Duncan. Duncan is the Scottish form of the Irish personal name Donagh. In Counties Derry and Donegal, Irish McDonagh was anglicised as Donaghy/Donaghey.

Surname	Rank	Origins
Robinson	53	Derived originally from the personal name Robert, a popular Old English personal name, Robinson is generally regarded as an English name and Robertson as a Scottish one. In Ulster, however, Robertson and Robinson have lost this neat distinction. In Perthshire, Clan Robertson took its name from their 15th century chief, Grizzled Robert. Clan Robertson was also known as Clan Donnachaidh. After the 1745 Jacobite Rising many Robertsons adopted the name Donachie which was further anglicised to Duncan. Members of Clan Robertson adopted this name after its 14th century chief, Fat Duncan. Duncan is the Scottish form of the Irish personal name Donagh. In Counties Derry and Donegal, Irish McDonagh was anglicised as Donaghy/Donaghey.
Roddy	169	*Irish*. There were two distinct septs of this name; one originating in County Leitrim and the other in Donegal. The latter were hereditary tenants of the church lands at Taughboyne. In some cases Roddy has become confused with the County Kilkenny sept name of Reddy.
Rodgers	188	Can be of *English, Scottish* or *Irish* origin. Derived from the Germanic personal name Roger this surname, meaning son of Rodger, was introduced to Britain by the Normans. In Ireland, McGrory and its variants such as McRory were anglicised to Rodgers.
Rooney	300	*Irish*. This County Down sept, with its homeland near Rathfriland, was noted, from the 11th century, for their literary prowess. Furthermore, the County Fermanagh sept of Mulrooney, Kings of Fermanagh before the Maguires, had their name shortened to Rooney.
Rosborough/ Rossborough	301	*Scottish*. In historical records Rosborough is variously recorded as Rosborrow, Rosebrough, Rosebrugh, Rossborough, Rossboro, Roxberry, Roxborough and Roxbrough. Derived from the town of Roxburgh in the Scottish Borders this surname was well-established, as Rosebrough and Rosebrugh, in the Claudy/Banagher area of County Derry by 1796. In 1831 census of County Derry, Rosboroughs were concentrated in the parishes of Cumber and Banagher and Roxboroughs in Aghadowey parish.
Ross	170	*English* and *Scottish*. Derived from various place names found throughout England. A Yorkshire family of the name settled in Ayrshire in the 12th century; a branch of whom, in turn, settled in County Down in the 17th century. In the North of Scotland, Clan Ross, with origins in the 13th century, took their name from the ancient Province of Ross.
Roulston	302	*English*. Derived from various place names found throughout England, meaning Rolf's farm.

Surname	Rank	Origins
Russell	251	*English* and *Scottish*. Derived from a nickname meaning 'red' this surname became quite widespread all over England and Scotland. In the Scottish Highlands the Russells were septs of Clans Buchanan and Cumming. A Norman family of the name came to County Down in the 12th century.
Rutherford	182	*Scottish*. Derived from the place name in Roxburghshire meaning ford of the horned cattle. On record since the 12th century the Rutherfords became one of the most powerful riding clans of the Scottish Borders.
Scott	183	*Scottish*. The term Scot originally referred to the Gaelic colonists from eastern Ulster, in the ancient Kingdom of Dal Riata, who had established themselves in Kintyre and Argyll by the beginning of the 6th century. Under increasing pressure from the expanding dynasties claiming descent from the 5th century High King of Ireland, Niall of the Nine Hostages, the peoples of east Ulster began to settle in Scotland. The Scotts, who acquired their lands in the 12th century, became one of the most powerful riding clans in the Scottish Borders who, at the height of their power in the 16th century, could muster an army of 600 men.
Semple	272	*English* and *Scottish*. Derived from a number of place names in Normandy called Saint-Paul, from the dedication of their churches to Saint Paul (the sword of Saint Paul has been part of the coat of arms of the city of Derry/Londonderry since 1613). A Scottish family of this name held the hereditary post of Sheriff of Renfrewshire from the 13th century.
Sharkey	161	*Irish*. This sept originated in County Tyrone as O'Sharkey but the prefix O was dropped by the 18th century.
Sheerin	234	*Irish*. There were two distinct septs of this name; one originating in Cork and the other in Donegal/Fermanagh. The former is now extinct while the latter spread as far south as County Leix.
Shiels/ Shields	78	Can be of *English*, *Scottish* or *Irish* origin. In England and Scotland it derived either from a local name for someone who lived by a shelter or shallow place or from an occupational name for a maker of shields. In Ireland the Shiels or Shields, with origins in Inishowen, County Donegal and tracing their descent from the 5th century High King of Ireland, Niall of the Nine Hostages were a sept of hereditary physicians. In Derry most Shields and Shiels will be of this origin.

Surname	Rank	Origins
Simpson	37	*English* and *Scottish*. Meaning son of Simon it was derived from the Old Testament name Simeon which became a very popular medieval first name. In Devon in the 13th century three places named Simpson gave rise to the surname there. In the Highlands of Scotland McKimmie, a sept of Clan Fraser, whose name meant son of Simon, was anglicised to Simpson. Simpson has been recorded in Ulster since the 17th century.
Smith	15	Smith, also spelt Smyth, can be of *English*, *Scottish* or *Irish* origin. It is the commonest surname in England, Scotland, Wales and Ulster. This occupational name sprang up all over England wherever there was a smith (such as blacksmith, gunsmith, goldsmith, etc.). In Scotland and Ireland Smith was a further anglicisation of McGowan.
Starrett/ Sterritt	219	*Scottish*. Derived from the Ayrshire place name of Stairaird (now known as Stirie) this name, variously spelt as Stirrat and Starrat, was once very common in the parish of Dalry in Ayrshire. In Ulster the name was spelt Starrett and Sterritt where it became well known in Donegal and adjacent areas. In a few cases it may be derived from English Start which was derived from a number of minor place names meaning a promontory.
Stevenson	189	*English* and *Scottish*. Meaning son of Steven it was derived from the personal name Stephen which was popularised by the Normans. Stevenson is usually regarded as the Scottish form of the name and Stephenson as the English. But this distinction is now largely blurred. Steenson and Stinson are variants of the name found only in Ulster. The Stevensons who settled in the Lurgan area in County Armagh in the 17th century were Quakers and/or linen weavers from England.
Stewart	38	*Scottish*. Derived from the Old English occupational name of Steward who was the keeper of a household. As every Bishop or Landlord had his Steward the name sprang up all over Scotland. From the 12th century Walter, the High Steward of the Royal household, who was responsible for the collection of taxes and the administration of justice, descended the Scottish Royal family of Stewart. Clan Stewart, which also traces its descent from the above Walter, later divided into separate clans: the Stewarts of Appin; of Atholl; of Bute; and of Galloway. Nine of the 59 Scottish 'undertakers' or landowners granted lands in the 17th century Plantation of Ulster were Stewarts.

Surname	Rank	Origins
Strawbridge	303	This name is very much associated with the Derry area and is probably *Scottish* in origin. Recorded as Strobridge and Strawbridge in the 1663 Hearth Money Rolls in Templemore and Cumber parishes respectively this name has been associated with the rural parishes, especially Glendermot parish, to the east of Derry city for well over 300 years.
Sweeney	68	*Scots Gaelic.* This sept was well established in Kintyre, Argyllshire by the year 1200. As one of the most renowned galloglass (mercenary soldier) families they settled in the Fanad peninsula, County Donegal from 1267 and over the subsequent four centuries they fought on the side of the O'Donnells.
Taggart	304	*Scots Gaelic.* Meaning son of the priest the Taggarts or McTaggarts were a sept of Clan Ross. The name became very common in Dumfriesshire. *Irish.* This County Fermanagh sept were hereditary tenants of church lands at Ballymacataggart in Derryvullan parish.
Taylor	43	*English* and *Scottish.* Derived from the occupational name of tailor. On the English side of the Scottish Borders the Tailors were one of the riding clans. In the Lowlands of Scotland the name was first recorded in the late 13th century while in the Highlands the Taylors or McTaylors were a sept of Clan Cameron in Argyllshire. The name was well known in Ireland from the 14th century but it was the 17th century Plantation of Ulster which established the name in great numbers in Counties Antrim, Down and Derry.
Temple	235	*English.* Derived from one of the houses, known as temples, maintained by the Knights Templar who, as a military crusading order, were active in the Middle East in the 12th century. In the thirty year period to 1755 no less than 104 foundlings baptised at the Temple Church, London were surnamed Temple or Templar. *Scottish.* Derived from the parish of Temple in Edinburgh which was the principal residence of the Knights Templar in Scotland.
Thompson	20	*English* and *Scottish.* Meaning son of Thomas this surname, spelt as Thompson, was the 15th commonest name in England and, as Thomson, was the 5th commonest in Scotland. This distinction in spelling, however, was not perpetuated in Ulster. The Thomsons were one of the lesser riding clans of the Scottish Borders; many of whom settled in County Fermanagh during the 17th century Plantation of Ulster. In the Highlands of Scotland a number of distinct septs of McThomas anglicised their name to Thomson and to McCombe and Holmes.

Surname	Rank	Origins
Tierney	252	*Irish.* There were three septs of this name, with the most important, who were Lords of Carra, originating in County Mayo. Today Tierney is chiefly associated with Counties Galway, Limerick and Tipperary. A small County Donegal sept of the name will, however, be the origin of most Derry Tierneys.
Toland	88	*Irish.* Originating in south Donegal many members of this sept migrated to Mayo with some of the leading O'Donnells in 1602. In Mayo they became better known as Tolan.
Tracey	117	*Irish.* There were at one time three distinct septs of this name: in Galway they were a branch of the O'Maddens; in Cork they were of the same stock as the O'Donovans; and in Leix the Traceys were Lords of Slievemargy.
Villa	305	This name is very much concentrated in the Derry area yet it is unrecorded anywhere in County Derry in 1831 census. This surname, however, is found in both Italy and Spain where it derived as a local name for someone who lived in a village.
Walker	41	*English* and *Scottish.* In the North and West of England Walker derived as an occupational name for a fuller. In the Middle Ages it was the fuller's job to scour and thicken raw cloth by 'walking' or trampling upon it in a trough filled with water. Walker also became widespread in Scotland where it was first recorded in the early 14th century. In Ireland the name is most common in counties Antrim, Down and Derry.
Wallace	132	*English* and *Scottish.* Meaning Welshman or Celt this term was applied by the conquering Normans to the native population of England and Wales. In Scotland, Wallace derived as a native name for a Strathclyde Briton. It first appeared in the 12th century in Ayrshire and Renfrewshire which were parts of the ancient Celtic Kingdom of Strathclyde. As Clan Wallace they acquired extensive lands in Ayrshire.
Walsh	118	*Irish.* Meaning Welshman this name, the fourth most numerous in Ireland, was given to many of the solider-adventurers who followed in the wake of the Anglo-Norman invasion of the late 12th century. As the name arose independently all over Ireland the Walshes didn't develop along sept lines. Walsh was gaelicised to *Breathnach* which in turn was anglicised to Brannagh and Brannick.

Surname	Rank	Origins
Ward	52	Can be of *English*, *Scottish* or *Irish* origin. In England this name derived as an occupational name for a watchman or guard. Most Wards in Ireland, however, are of Gaelic Irish origin. Meaning son of the bard, and also anglicised as McAward and McWard, septs of this name were hereditary poets to both the O'Kellys of Galway and the O'Donnells of Donegal. The Wards of Donegal were based at Lettermacaward near Glenties. In Scotland McWard generally became Baird but not Ward.
Watson	141	*English* and *Scottish*. Meaning son of Watt, which in turn was derived from the Old German name Walter, this name became most numerous in Aberdeenshire and Banffshire. In the Highlands of Scotland Watt, McWatt and Watson have become confused as the Watt septs attached to Clans Buchanan and Forbes also anglicised their name to Watson.
White	79	Can be of *English*, *Scottish* or *Irish* origin. In England and the Lowlands of Scotland this name derived as a nickname for someone with 'fair hair' or 'fair complexion'. In the Scottish Highlands White was one of the colour names adopted by members of Clans MacGregor and Lamont on their proscription in the 17th century. In Ireland those names which contained the Gaelic epithet ban or gael, meaning white, such as Bane, Bawn, Kilbane and Galligan were frequently anglicised to White.
Whoriskey	253	*Irish*. Recorded in County Roscommon in 1591 as O'Fworishe this sept name was anglicised in Donegal to Whoriskey in the first instance and then to Waters and Watters. Several Irish names such as Hiskey, Whoriskey and Toorish were anglicised to Waters.
Williams	184	*English* and *Scottish*. Meaning son of William it was derived from the Old German personal name William which was introduced to Britain by the Normans. Williams became an extremely common surname in England and Wales whereas, in Scotland, Williamson, as opposed to Williams, was more favoured. Furthermore the Highlands' name of McWilliams, with septs of this name attached to Clans Gunn and MacFarlane, was anglicised to Williamson.
Wilson	25	*English* and *Scottish*. Derived from the Old German personal name William which was introduced to Britain by the Normans. It is estimated that 80% of Ulster Wilsons are of Scottish descent; Wilson was a common name throughout the Lowlands of Scotland. Furthermore the Wilsons were septs of Clan Gunn in Caithness and Sutherland and of Clan Innes in Banffshire.

Surname	Rank	Origins
Wood/ Woods	306	Can be *English*, *Scottish* or *Irish* in origin. In England and Scotland Wood, a common surname in both countries, derived as a local name for someone who lived in or near a wood. Woods, however, is a rather uncommon name in Britain. By contrast in Ireland, Woods is ten times more numerous than Wood and most will be of Gaelic Irish stock. A number of sept names such as McEnhill and McElhone of Tyrone, Coyle and McIlhoyle of Donegal and Kielty of Down were anglicised to Woods. Wood and Woods are, therefore, two distinct names although the passage of time will have blurred this distinction.
Wray	162	*English*. This name is especially associated with Yorkshire where it derived from a number of minor place names in northern England meaning nook or remote place. In the 16th century a Yorkshire family named Wray did settle in the Derry area. Not only has Wray become confused with Rea it has, in some instances, become Rowe. In Ulster, names such as O'Rawe and Reagh were anglicised to Rea while Scottish McCrae was abbreviated to Rea.
Wright	206	Can be of *English*, *Scottish* or *Irish* origin. In northern England and the Lowlands of Scotland Wright derived as an occupational name for a carpenter or joiner. In the Highlands of Scotland the Wrights were a sept of Clan McIntyre while in Ireland McAteer, a County Armagh sept, meaning son of the carpenter, was anglicised to Wright.
Wylie	111	*English*. Derived from a number of different place names such as Willey meaning willow wood or River Wiley meaning tricky river, i.e. a river liable to flood. *Scottish*. In Ulster Wylie is more likely to be of Scottish origin. Wylie is a common name in Scotland where it was derived from the personal name William. It was recorded in Dumfriesshire in the late 14th century.
Young	71	*English* and *Scottish*. Derived as a nickname to distinguish father and son with the same christian name. In England this name was most numerous in County Durham and in the South West of the country. The Youngs of Culdaff, County Donegal originated from Devon. The Youngs were one of the lesser riding clans of the Scottish Borders. In Ireland the gaelic epithet Og, meaning young, which frequently accompanied Irish forenames sometimes gave rise to the surname Young.

Appendix 1

The Family History of Ireland in 132 Generations from 'The Creation' to Ramon 'O Dogherty of Inishowen, Chief of the Name'

Historical Background

Dr Ramon Salvador O'Dogherty of San Fernando, near Cadiz, Spain was inaugurated on 17 July 1990 as the 37th O'Dochartaigh, Chief of Inishowen. Fergus Gillespie of the Office of the Chief Herald in Dublin, compiled for Derry Genealogy (www.rootsireland.ie/derry-genealogy) for the Irish Homecoming Festival in September 1992, a chart which, on the male line, recorded the ancestors of Ramon O'Dogherty, "Chief of the Name", back through 46 generations to Niall of the Nine Hostages.

The founder of the Spanish branch of the O'Dohertys was John who, on the death of his father Eoghan in 1784, came out with his brothers Henry and Clinton Dillon to pursue a career in the Spanish Navy, the most exclusive branch of the Spanish armed forces. Entry required them to show their genealogy, proving noble origin. In 1790 the King of Arms in Dublin Castle confirmed the three brothers as being "descended in a direct line from Shane or Sir John O'Dogherty, Chief of Innish-Owen".

The Genealogical Office manuscript collections (GO Ms) in the Office of the Chief Herald at the National Library of Ireland, Dublin (http://www.nli.ie/en/heraldry-introduction.aspx) are the most important source for the genealogies of Gaelic families and of those families entitled to bear arms either by hereditary right of by grant.

Pre-Christian Genealogies

In pre-Christian Ireland the exploits and genealogies of the Celts were preserved orally, in verse and song, by the poets or *Filidh* who were the custodians of the ancient traditions of the tribal groups. The introduction of writing, fixed to a large extent, these tales of tribal myth, origin-legend and genealogical descent.

The central characters of Ireland's sagas now found their way into genealogies as the remote ancestors of the dynasties and tribes who emerged triumphant in the 7th century AD. Gaelic genealogies were essentially political. When new tribal or dynastic groups rose to power and overthrew a ruling dynasty, the genealogists often forged a link between them and their predecessors and in this way continuity and legitimacy were assured.

In Ireland, the ancient genealogists endowed the ruling dynasties with pedigrees of kings and warriors with origin-legends in pagan times. They also constructed genealogies which connected with Christian tradition and history as revealed in the Bible. Thus the genealogies of the emerging tribal or dynastic groups were extended back to Noah and to Adam and Eve.

The main body of genealogical lore and of saga literature of early Ireland were preserved in a series of manuscripts, written from the 12th century in a mixture of Latin and Gaelic, but in many cases these were copies of tales written down for the first time in the 6th or 7th century AD.

The end result is that pedigrees were constructed which take the origins of Niall of the Nine Hostages back through 86 generations, on the male line, to 'The Creation' and to Adam and Eve. *The Annals of The Kingdom of Ireland by the Four Masters* (a chronicle of Irish history from 'the earliest period to the year 1616') dated 'The Creation', based on biblical chronology, as 5194 BC.

Much of this information was condensed and published in two volumes by John O'Hart with the title: *IRISH PEDIGREES; or, THE ORIGIN AND STEM of THE IRISH NATION.* (Fifth Edition published Dublin, 1892 and Reprinted by Genealogical Publishing Company, Baltimore, 1976.)

I have always been amazed by the sheer volume of genealogical, mythical and historical detail, and by the breadth of vision recorded in O'Hart's *Irish Pedigrees*. In particular, it is fascinating to see places of recognised historical importance such as Grianan of Aileach, the Hill of Tara and Navan Fort, and of stories from Celtic mythology about celebrated warriors such as Maeve, Finn McCool and Cuchulainn woven into the many pedigrees recorded in his book.

Indeed the major Gaelic clans of the Highlands of Scotland such as the MacDonalds and Campbells are also an offshoot of this family tree; i.e. from the 2nd century Conn of the Hundred Battles, King of Connacht.

Using O'Hart's work I have summarised the family history of Niall of the Nine Hostages back to Adam and Eve in a family tree which was called by O'Hart, *The Stem of the Irish Nation.* This family tree, by connecting with Ireland's rich saga lore and with Christian tradition as revealed in the Bible, brings together Celtic mythology, history, genealogical descent and stories from the Bible.

Hence in 132 steps – in 46 generations from Ramon O'Dogherty, "Chief of the Name" of Inishowen, County Donegal to Niall of the Nine Hostages, High King of Ireland 379-405 AD, and in a further 86 generations from Niall of the Nine Hostages to Adam and Eve – the family tree in this section charts the family history of Ireland.

The Family History of Ireland in 132 Generations from 'The Creation' to Ramon 'O Dogherty of Inishowen, Chief of the Name'

ADAM and EVE

The Annals of The Kingdom of Ireland by the Four Masters (a chronicle of Irish history from 'the earliest period to the year 1616') dates the Creation as 5194 BC.

|

SETH

|

ENOS

|

CAINAN

|

MAHALALEEL

|

JARED

|

ENOCH

|

METHUSELAH

|

LAMECH

|

NOAH

The Annals of The Kingdom of Ireland dates the Flood, referred to as "the Deluge", as 2952 BC.
Noah divided the world amongst his three sons: Asia to Shem; Arabia and Africa to Ham; and Europe to Japhet.

|

JAPHET

The oldest son of Noah. He had 15 sons, amongst whom he divided Europe

|

MAGOG

|

BAOTH

Granted Scythia, an ancient Kingdom in Southeast Europe

|

PHOENIUSA FARSAIDH
King of Scythia

|

NIUL

Invited into Egypt by the Pharaoh and granted land near the Red Sea

|
|
|

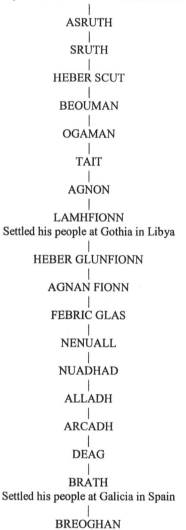

GAODHAL

Moses cured Gaodhal in his youth of a snake bite in his neck. Gaodhal was the ancestor of the *Clan-na-Gael*, i.e. "the children or descendants of Gaodhal"

ASRUTH

SRUTH

HEBER SCUT

BEOUMAN

OGAMAN

TAIT

AGNON

LAMHFIONN
Settled his people at Gothia in Libya

HEBER GLUNFIONN

AGNAN FIONN

FEBRIC GLAS

NENUALL

NUADHAD

ALLADH

ARCADH

DEAG

BRATH
Settled his people at Galicia in Spain

BREOGHAN
Conquered Spain and Portugal and established a colony in northern England

BILE

MILESIUS

Defended Egypt on behalf of the Pharaoh against the King of Ethiopia. Milesius then returned to Spain before a famine drove him westwards to fulfil a Druidic prophecy that their Nomadic way of life would not end until they arrived at "the Western Island of Europe", now called Ireland. **The conquest of Ireland and defeat of the Tuatha-de-Danans,** earlier invaders of Ireland, was completed by his sons by 1699 BC.

HEBER FIONN	HEREMON	IR
From whom descend the Kings of Munster. **The Rock of Cashel** rising from the Tipperary Plain was the seat of the Kings of Munster from 370 until 1101 AD.	The seventh son of Milesius. From him descend the Kings of Connacht, Dalriada and Leinster, and the Kings of Scotland. Heremon and Heber became joint monarchs of Ireland in 1699 BC The **Hill of Tara** was the Seat of the High Kings of Ireland until it was abandoned in 1022 AD.	His descendants settled in Ulster. Conor MacNeasa, King of Ulster, who was in continual war with Queen Maedhbh of Connacht, was of the Line of Ir. **Emain Macha** (Navan Fort) was the seat of the Kings of Ulster.

IRIAL FAIDH
10th Monarch of Ireland, died 1670 BC

EITHRIAL

FOLL-AICH

TIGERNMAS

ENBOATH

SMIOMGHALL
In his reign the Picts in Scotland were forced to pay homage to the Irish Monarch

FIACHA LABHRAINN

AONGUS OLMUCACH
20th Monarch of Ireland from 1427 to 1409 BC. Went to Scotland with a strong army and forced
the Picts, after 30 battles, to pay tribute to him

|

MAIN

|

ROTHEACHTACH

|

DEIN

|

SIORNA

|

OLIOLL AOLCHEOIN

|

GIALCHADH

|

NUADHAS FIONNFAIL
39th Monarch of Ireland. Slain in 961 BC

|

AEDAN GLAS
During his reign a plague swept away most of the population

|

SIMEON BREAC

|

MUREDACH BOLGACH

|

FIACHA TOLGRACH

|

DUACH LADHRACH

|

EOCHAIDH BUADHACH

|

UGAINE MOR
66th Monarch of Ireland from 633 to 593 BC (contemporary with Alexander the Great). He was
called Mor (i.e. Great) because he was sovereign of all "the Islands of Western Europe". He had
25 children, and to prevent these children encroaching on each other he divided his kingdom in
Ireland into 25 portions.

|

COLETHACH CAOL-BHREAGH

|

MELG MOLBHTHACH

|

|

|

IARAN GLEOFATHACH

|

CONLA CAOMH
|
OLIOLL CAS-FIACHLACH
|
EOCHAIDH ALT-LEATHAN
|
AONGUS TUIRMEACH-TEAMRACH
Slain at Tara in 324 BC. His son Fiach Firmara was ancestor of the
Kings of Dalriada and Argyll in Scotland.
|
ENNA AIGNEACH
|
ASSAMAN EAMHNA
|
ROIGHEN RUADH
|
FIONNLOGH
|
FIONN
|
EOCHAIDH FEIDLIOCH

93rd Monarch of Ireland from 142 to 130 BC. Died at Tara in 130 BC. He resumed the ancient division of Ireland into Provinces, namely Two Munsters, Leinster, Connacht and Ulster. His daughter Maedhbh, Queen of Connacht, led an army into Ulster on the **Cattle Raid of Cooley**. "The Ulster Cycle", the oldest heroic literature in Europe, outside the classical world, tells of the deeds in warfare of Conor MacNeasa, King of Ulster and his Red Branch Knights, especially **Cuchulainn**, Ulster's greatest champion, against their mortal enemies the people of Connacht under the warrior-queen Maedhbh (Maeve).

BRESS-NAR-LOTHAR
|
LUGHAIDH SRIABH-n DEARG

98th Monarch of Ireland from 34 to 8 BC. He entered into an alliance with the King of Denmark through marriage to his daughter.

CRIMTHANN-NIADH-NAR

100th Monarch of Ireland. Jesus Christ was born during his reign. He made expeditions to Britain and Gaul and assisted the Picts and Britons in their wars with the Romans.

FEREDACH FIONN-FEACHTNACH
Died at Tara in 36 AD.
|
FIACHA FIONN OLA
|
|
|

TUATHAL TEACHTMAR

106th Monarch of Ireland. From each of the fours provinces of Ireland he took a considerable tract of land and created, as the Monarch's own demesne, the new territory of Midhe or Meath. Slain in 106 AD.

|

FEDHLIMIDH RACHTMAR

108th Monarch of Ireland from 110 to 119 A.D. He married Ughna, daughter of the King of Denmark.

|

|

|

CONN CEADCATHACH or **CONN OF THE HUNDRED BATTLES**

This Conn, King of Connacht, was so-called from hundreds of battles fought and won against the Kings of Munster, Leinster and Ulster. 110th Monarch of Ireland from 123 to 157 AD. Assassinated in Tara in 157 AD by 50 men, disguised as women, on the orders of the King of Ulster. According to Clan Donald genealogical lore the MacDonalds of Scotland trace their ancestry to Conn of the Hundred Battles. At the Battle of Harlaw in 1411 the Clan Donald war cry proclaimed:

O Children of Conn of the Hundred Battles.
Now is the time for you to win recognition

Conn's brother Fiacha Suidhe was ancestor of Diarmuid Ua Duibhne, founder of Clan Campbell of Scotland.

|

ART EANFHEAR

|

CORMAC ULFHADA or CORMAC Mac ART

115th Monarch of Ireland from 226 to 266 AD. Fionn Mac Cumhaill (i.e. Finn McCool), the celebrated warrior, was the son-in-law of Cormac MacArt. **Finn McCool**, who was slain near the Boyne in 283 AD, led the Fianna, a select band of warriors, who upheld the power of the High King.

|

CAIRBRE-LIFEACHAR

|

FIACHA SRABHTEINE

King of Connacht and 120th Monarch of Ireland from 285 to 322 AD. He was slain by his nephews, the Three Collas, in 322 AD. The Three Collas are reputed to have burnt Emain Macha (Navan Fort) and driven the Ulaid, i.e. the Ulstermen, eastwards. Archaeological evidence suggests Navan Fort was ritually burnt to the ground in the First Century BC.

|

MUIREADACH TIREACH

Regained the monarchy of Ireland from the Three Collas by defeating Colla Uais in 326 AD. Colla Uais and his two brothers were now banished to Scotland. From Colla Uais descend the MacDonalds, Lords of the Isles and chiefs of Glencoe.

|

|

|EOCHAIDH MUIGH-MEADHOIN
124th Monarch of Ireland from 357 to 365 AD

|

NIALL MOR or **NIALL OF THE NINE HOSTAGES**

King of Tara. Monarch of Ireland from 379 to 405 AD. Renowned for his expeditions against the Romans in Britain and Gaul. On one of his raids the young St Patrick was captured and brought to Ireland. Slain 405 AD.

In the 5th century AD Niall's fourteen sons began to expand eastwards and northwards out of Connacht, taking sword land as far north as Inishowen, County Donegal. The conquest of north-western Ulster, and the capturing of the great prehistoric dry-stone stronghold at **Grianan of Aileach** about 425 AD, is assigned to four of Niall's sons, namely Eoghan, Conall Gulban, Enda and Cairbre.

Eoghan established his own kingdom in the peninsula still called after him Inishowen (Innis Eoghain or Eoghan's Isle) between Lough Swilly and Lough Foyle. Eoghan was converted to Christianity by St Patrick at Grianan of Aileach about 442 AD. Conal Gulban was slain in battle in 464 AD, and his brother Eoghan, "died of grief for Conal Gulban", in 465 AD.

The by-product of this northward expansion by the descendants of Niall of the Nine Hostages was the pushing out of the existing peoples of the Kingdom of Dal Riada in Ulster across the Irish Channel to Argyll, Scotland and the founding of the Kingdom of Scots about 490 AD.

|

Conall Gulban
from whom descend
Cenel Conaill (the Race of Conall)
a branch of the Northern Ui Neill

|

Fergus Cendfota

|

Setnae

|

Lugaid

|

Ronan

|

Garb

|

Cenn Faelad

|

Fiaman
from whom descend
Clann Fiamhain

|

Maengal

|

Dochartach
from whom is the surname
O Dochartaigh (O'Dogherty, O'Doherty, Doherty etc.)

Maengal

Donnchad

Maengal

Domnall Droma Fornochta

Donnchad Donn

Domnall Finn

Conchobar

Diarmait

Muirchertach

Aengus

Domnall Mor

Ruaidri

Domnall

Conchobar Manach

Aindiles

Domnall
Lord of Ard Miodhair and Tir Eanna
(in barony of Raphoe)
d. 1342

Sean
Lord of Ard Miodhair
d. 1359

Conchobar an Einigh
Lord of Inishowen and Ard Miodhair
m. Maire, daughter of O Cathain (O'Kane, O'Cahan)
d. 1413
|
Domhnall
Lord of Ard Miodhair
m. Cobhlaigh, daughter of Aodh Dubh O Domhnaill (O'Donnell), King of Tir Chonaill
d. 1440
|
Brian Dubh
Lord
d. 1496
|
Conchobhar Carrach
Lord
d. 1516
|
Feidhlim
Lord
d. 1556
|
Sean Mor
Lord of Inishowen
m. Aibhilin, daughter of Mag Uidhir (Maguire), Lord of Fermanagh
d. 1582
|
Sir Sean Og
Lord of Inishowen
m. daughter of "Shane the Proud" O Neill (O'Neill), King of Tir Eoghain
d. 1601

|
Sir Cathaoir
Lord of Inishowen
m. Mary, daughter of Christopher Preston,
Viscount Gormanston
Killed near Kilmacrenan in war with English 1608

Sean
m. Aislinn, daughter of
Padraig O Cathain of Derry

Eoghan
m. Maire, daughter of Conchobhar O Ruairc (O'Rourke), Lord of Breifne Ui Ruairc
d. 1642

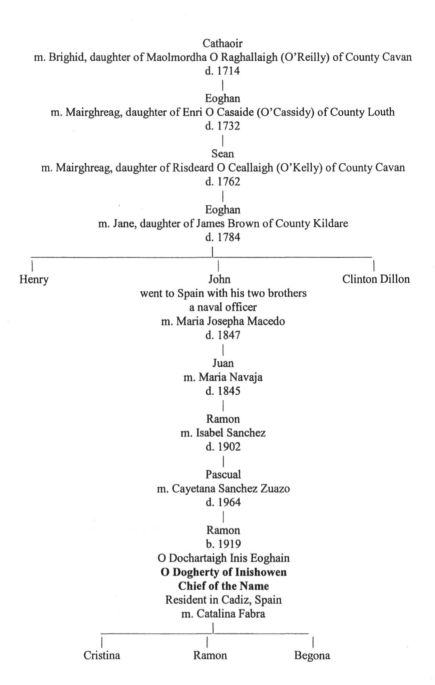

Cathaoir
m. Brighid, daughter of Maolmordha O Raghallaigh (O'Reilly) of County Cavan
d. 1714

Eoghan
m. Mairghreag, daughter of Enri O Casaide (O'Cassidy) of County Louth
d. 1732

Sean
m. Mairghreag, daughter of Risdeard O Ceallaigh (O'Kelly) of County Cavan
d. 1762

Eoghan
m. Jane, daughter of James Brown of County Kildare
d. 1784

Henry

John
went to Spain with his two brothers
a naval officer
m. Maria Josepha Macedo
d. 1847

Clinton Dillon

Juan
m. Maria Navaja
d. 1845

Ramon
m. Isabel Sanchez
d. 1902

Pascual
m. Cayetana Sanchez Zuazo
d. 1964

Ramon
b. 1919
O Dochartaigh Inis Eoghain
O Dogherty of Inishowen
Chief of the Name
Resident in Cadiz, Spain
m. Catalina Fabra

Cristina

Ramon

Begona

Printed in the USA
CPSIA information can be obtained
at www.ICGtesting.com
CBHW070945071024
15412CB00004B/24

9 780806 358420